Mapping the Croatian Coast

A Road Trip to Architectural Legacies of Cold War and Tourism Boom

...d by
...Krejs

With contributions by
Irena Atanasova
Carina Bliem
Nataša Bodrožić
Lidija Butković Mićin
Diana Contiu
Melita Čavlović
Antonia Dika
Magdalena Drach
Lucia de la Duena Sotelo
Aline Eriksson
Michaela Fodor
Sarah Gold
Raphael Gregorits
Joana Gritsch
Maria Groiss
Nina Haider
Pia Knott
Bernadette Krejs
Cristina Krois
Michael Obrist
Philip Langer
Michael Lindinger
Jakob Lugmayr
Nina Zawosta
Michael Zinganel
Marija Živanović

jovis

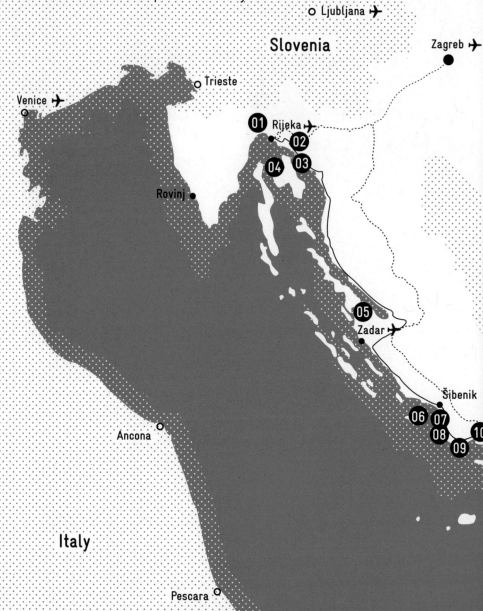

Mapping the Croatian Coast
A Road Trip along Jadranska Magistrala
675 km - 17 stops - 5 days

Slovenia

Ljubljana ✈

Zagreb ✈

Trieste

Venice ✈

01 Rijeka ✈

02

03

04

Rovinj

05

Zadar ✈

Šibenik

06 **07**

08 **1C**

09

Áncona

Italy

Pescara

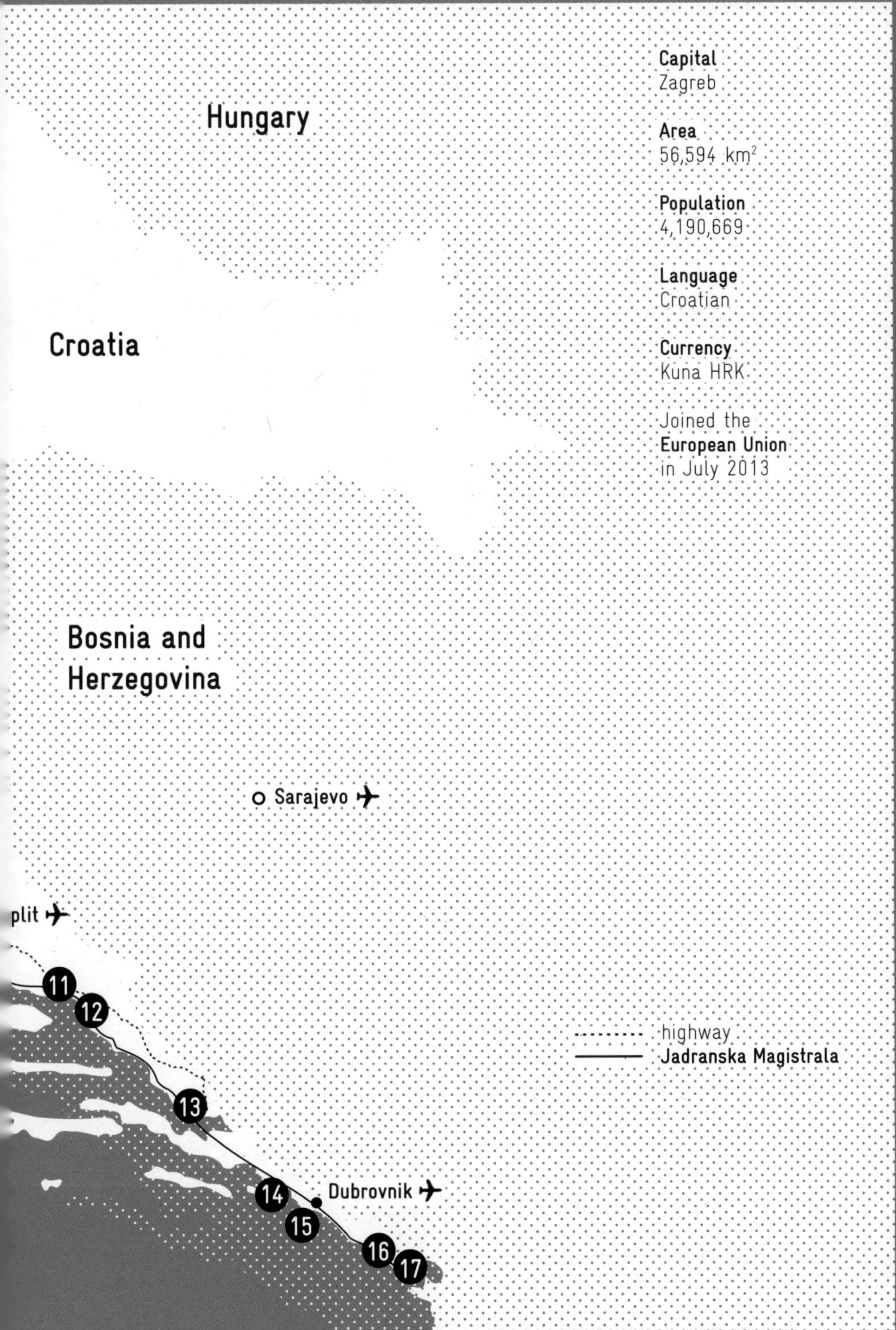

Hungary

Croatia

Bosnia and
Herzegovina

o Sarajevo ✈

plit ✈

11
12

13

14
Dubrovnik ✈
15

16 **17**

Capital
Zagreb

Area
56,594 km^2

Population
4,190,669

Language
Croatian

Currency
Kuna HRK

Joined the
European Union
in July 2013

········· highway
———— Jadranska Magistrala

Index

II.
Mappings

I.
Reader

Mapping the Croatian Coast

5 days, 17 locations and 675 kilometres
In October 2018, we set out on a road trip with 22 architecture students of TU Vienna and an old Croatia Lines bus. From Rijeka to Dubrovnik along "Jadranska Magistrala" – the picturesque coastal road built in the 1960s. Between the sea and the karstic backlands, we visited formerly prestigious buildings of Yugoslav tourism architecture as well as once strictly secret defence facilities of the Cold War: military barracks, ship bunkers, huge hotel complexes and motel bungalows – all built during the same time period and many of them vacant today, yet set on highly attractive coastal building plots.

Our research method: collective mapping. Out of the bus windows, along the entire Adriatic Highway, we recorded numerous characteristics, including gas stations, snack bars, schools, Hajduk Split graffiti and many more. At every location we visited, we examined the site's current condition, its infrastructure and accessibility, we analysed the ways it was embedded in the landscape and searched for traces of its reuse. Along the road, we tried to figure out the complex circumstances revolving around this precious architectural heritage.

Back in Vienna, with 15 kilograms of tangerines from the Neretva valley in our luggage, we asked ourselves what we had learned from the Croatian Coast with all its spatial, but also social, economic and legal determinants. Topics like temporary housing, the influence of seasonality, changing mobility, as well as ruins as an architecture that no longer fulfills its original purpose in its original form lingered. What significance do these visible and invisible architectures of tourism and the military have today, and how do they shape the landscape and future development of the region?
Some answers, ideas and suggestions concerning these questions can be found in the publication "Mapping the Croatian Coast".

A Road Trip to Architectural Legacies of Cold War and Tourism Boom

This book will accompany you, in the form of a travel guide, through the architectural heritage of the times of tourism boom and the Cold War. It directs you to selected locations and describes their genesis, their role in the non-aligned state of Yugoslavia, and their decline and transformation until today.

The guide comes with six essays: Michael Zinganel portrays the evolution of Yugoslav post-war tourism architecture and its transformation "from social tourism to a mass market consumer paradise". Melita Čavlović discusses the conditions surrounding the construction of Jadranska Magistrala, the coastal road which was crucial for the development of the region and which provides this book with its itinerary. In their essay, Nataša Bodrožić & Lidija Butković Mićin present the valuable work behind the "Motel Trogir" initiative, which has contributed greatly to the appreciation and protection of late-modernist architecture in Croatia. Antonia Dika gives an overview of the simultaneous development of the eastern Adriatic coast in the service of both tourism and the military, and Bernadette Krejs describes the methodology of this book, "mapping as a research method in architecture".

Eight additional folding maps will help to understand issues like seasonality and mobility on the Croatian coast; they were designed by architecture students of the Faculty of Architecture and Planning [Research Unit of Housing and Design] at the Technical University in Vienna. The maps investigate distinctive phenomena of the coastal area, and their diverse visual representations demonstrate that mapping not only has the potential to precisely identify the status quo, but is also a suitable tool for imagining alternatives and for suggesting new potentials.

The publication "Mapping the Croatian Coast" serves as an attempt to preserve this valuable architectural heritage without necessarily conserving it, but rather by thinking beyond the present to envisage its future history.

—
Antonia Dika & Bernadette Krejs
Vienna 2020

"For the first time now, masses of people were able to see the multitude of coastal towns that before had only been accessible by sea from the other side, from the mainland, and from the safety of a car."

Melita Čavlović
Opposing Ambitions Shaping the Ground of the Eastern Adriatic Coast, p. 104–107

photo Philip Langer

Coastal Tour Meditations
Michael Obrist

Michael Obrist
[*1972, Bolzano, Italy]
is an architect and partner
of feld72 architecture and
urban strategies. Since
2018, he is professor for
housing and design and
director of the Research
Unit of Housing and Design
/ Institute of Architecture
and Design at the Technical
University of Vienna. He
has taught at various
universities and academies,
e.g. University of the
Arts Linz, Architectural
Association Visiting School
Slovenia, Salzburg Summer
Academy of Fine Arts,
School of Architecture
Bergen/Norway, TU Graz.
The work of feld72 has
been shown in the major
exhibitions for architecture
and urbanism worldwide,
i.e. Biennale di Venezia
2016, 2011, 2010, 2008,
2004, International
Architecture Biennial São
Paulo 2007, Architecture
Biennale Rotterdam 2003

[1] Michel de Certeau,
Practice of Everyday Life
(Berkley: University of
California Press, 1984), 92.

" Now, the roving gambler he was very bored
Trying to create a next world war
He found a promoter who nearly fell off the floor
He said, 'I never engaged in this kind of thing before
But yes, I think it can be very easily done
We'll just put some bleachers out in the sun
And have it on Highway 61' "

Bob Dylan,
Highway 61 revisited

It was not a small step from the campaign "Why haven't we seen a photograph of the whole Earth yet?" launched by Steward Brand in 1965, to the invention of Google Earth, though both were searching for an instrument and strategy to comprehend the complexity and unity of the world. Whilst the first images of the Earth caused an immediate impact, and the interconnectedness of the whole world suddenly dawned on people, with Google Earth we observe the reverse phenomenon.
The small image of the globe on our screens obscures the outrageousness of its program's ability to show a large part of the complexity and variety behind unity at any scale. The following words are said to have been engraved above the entrance of Plato's Academy: "Medeis ageometretos eisito." [Those who are ignorant of geometry may not enter this place.] With the knowledge of geometry in the Platonic sense, we can try to decipher the pattern we recognise from above. But the illusion of objectivity the view from above of satellites and planners confers of satellites and the planners is an elitist and deceptive one: it was the perspective of the gods and goddesses.

Michel de Certeau writes about the viewpoint of the observer from the top of the former Twin Towers of New York: "His elevation transfigures him into a voyeur. It puts him at a distance. It transforms the bewitching world by which one was 'possessed' into a text that lies before one's eyes. It allows one to read it, to be a solar Eye, looking down like a god. The exaltation of a scopic and gnostic drive: the fiction of knowledge is related to this lust to be a viewpoint and nothing more." [1]

Our urban agglomerations, which could once easily be called the 'city' (whereas today we have to invent new words), are still the most socially, culturally and technologically complex artefact mankind has invented. Today, the development of our built environment and new technologies of zenithal perception has brought us an epistemological dilemma. The more we observe from above, the less we seem to understand. In the manifestation of the chaos of late 20th century urbanism, like in the Rorschach inkblot test, we are convinced we recognise certain shapes, when in fact, it tells us more about ourselves and our starting points of perception. Territories of amnesia, schizophrenic landscapes, hysterical cities, all searching for a definition of their new identity. In this past century of the most rapid acceleration in the history of mankind, the world has changed, even where its form seems to have remained the same. From the rapid transformations of China and Dubai to the global success of gated communities and the unstoppable spread of slums within huge agglomerations in parts of South America, Africa and Asia – apparently nothing escapes the satellite's gaze. From above, we can see the 'cementation' of power and authority, the substantial manifestations of production relationships, the inscribed cultural manifestations and constructions of landscape, but often what is most essential escapes our view: Life within Forms. To understand the transformation of software in our built hardware, we have to dig deeper, amplifying our methods, trying to understand 'context' in the broadest possible sense. We have to immerge in the labyrinth of daily (urban) life without allowing ourselves to be deluded by the tricks of Daedalus, as Michel de Certeau reminds us in "The Practice of Everyday Life". Space is not a neutral box. Space is the result of social relations and cultural techniques. Without knowing the different codes and rituals of the different societies we are operating with(in), we will be always "lost in translation". Jean Baudrillard understood that the key for understanding the society of the United States was (the abundance of) space, and the cognitive tool to realize this was the car: "the point is not to write the sociology or psychology of the car, the point is to drive. That way you can learn more about this society than all academia could ever tell you." [2]

When Bernadette Krejs and Antonia Dika started their tour together with the students of the TU Vienna with the intent to map the Croatian coast, it was the space to be traversed itself that became the teacher for specific strategies, tactics and new ways of perceiving and conceiving architecture. The Adriatic Sea shapes the geography in an objective and non-political way – in the relation between the height of the sea level and the relative height of the topography of the landscape. Water and earth. It is human history that transformed these spaces on the Croatian, Italian or Slovenian coasts. Space and

[2] Jean Baudrillard, America (New York / London: Verso, 1989), 54.

[3] Vilém Flusser, "Planning the unplannable," in The Freedom of the Migrant: Objections to Nationalism, ed. Anke K. Finger (Chicago: University of Illinois Press, 2003), 28.

Place. Chora and Topos, as defined from antique philosophy. All the northern Mediterranean coasts became landscapes of desire with the invention of tourism. An artificial arcadia, constructed along the coastlines of the Adriatic Sea as the spatial equivalent of an eternal ludic and lazy Sunday for our exhausted bodies and minds, which are absorbed in the production processes of the economic system for the rest of the year. It seems that there was no difference in that regard between the capitalist and the communist system: exhaustion seems to be the "natural" final stage before holidays. Far away seem the days when "employment" in the latin word "negotium" was defined as the "negation of otium", thus the negation of "leisure" and "peace" – and not vice versa.

In his book "The Freedom of the Migrant: Objections to Nationalism", Vilém Flusser writes in his essay "Planning the Unplannable" that "tourism is travel for travel's sake" and suggests that at present, tourism plays a role that is more or less analogous to the one played by theory in antiquity: "Theory is a little like sightseeing (being a spectator of the sight-worthy), and classical theory differs from its modern counterpart in that it is pure – it was never its purpose to be applied. Modern tourism and classical theory have in common a gratuitous purposelessness as catharsis." [3]

But it was not only the thousands of migrants crossing the Mediterranean Sea in fragile boats in the last decades hoping for a better life, that distorted the idea of the Adriatic Coast as a collective temporary Elysium. It was also the return of the perception of the coastline as a border and defence line in former Yugoslavia that created a new imbalance. Whereas the Mediterranean Sea is today once more perceived as the ultimate European Border with Frontex (the European Border and Coast Guard Agency) at work, and the European public opinion is polarized when it comes to the permeability of that border, the geopolitical reality of the states of former Yugoslavia meant that landscapes of tourism and desire overlapped with the landscapes of war and fear a few decades before. Bernadette Krejs and Antonia Dika, together with the students of TU Vienna, used this phenomena on their starting point for their tour along the Croatian coast. Their projects are an attempt to start from the dichotomy of these two phenomena – aiming to arrive at new potentials and other possible worlds. The study of the established body of knowledge of various disciplines is combined with a "theory through praxis" in which the experiment seems to be the only possible response to the new conditions of contemporary space, because there are no users' manuals around to follow. A new discourse is formed on the margins of the disciplines, the emergence of a new practice, which is grounded not only in the broad tradition of knowledge of classical architecture schools, but amplified by the experience of different cultural strategies and tactics. In the understanding of reality through travelling and real-site experience, in the overlapping of architecture and new strategies and tactics, we leave traces in the material world, which the "eyes of the gods" can see, but cannot understand. Because the key to the understanding of our priviledge as human beings may lie in a reinterpretation of the old Latin proverb: "errare humanum est." [Making mistakes / wandering around is human.]

See also:
Michael Obrist, "Von göttlichen Augen und menschlichem Irren. Raumphänomene in Zeiten von Google Earth," in food&grid. raum&designstrategien, ed. Elsa Prochazka (2009), 37–42.

Michael Obrist, "Trojan Horses and other social animals", in Space Matters Chronicles, ed. Lukas Feireiss (Wien / NewYork: Springer, 2013), 106-107.

‹›
photo
Research Unit of Housing and Design

Timeline Croatia
1940–2019
history•tourism•military•privatisation•politics

Illustration by
Lucia De la Duena Sotelo and
Philip Langer

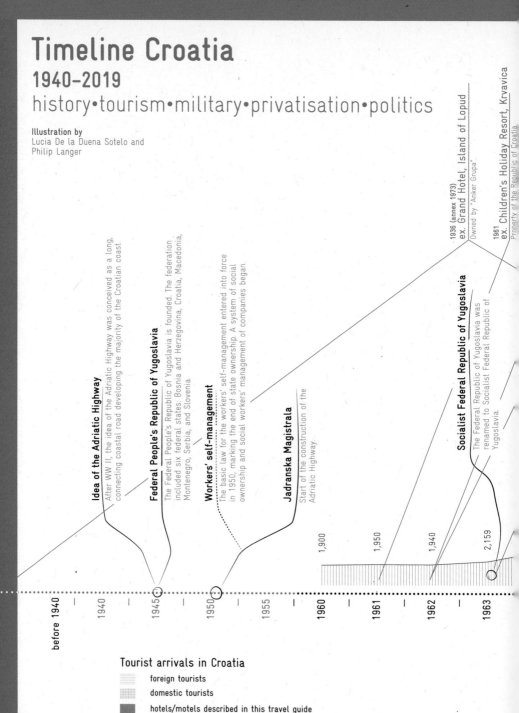

1936 (annex 1973)
ex. Grand Hotel, Island of Lopud
Owned by "Anker Grupa"

1961
ex. Children's Holiday Resort, Krvavica
Property of the Republic of Croatia

Idea of the Adriatic Highway
After WW II, the idea of the Adriatic Highway was conceived as a long, connecting coastal road developing the majority of the Croatian coast.

Federal People's Republic of Yugoslavia
The Federal People's Republic of Yugoslavia is founded. The federation included six federal states: Bosnia and Herzegovina, Croatia, Macedonia, Montenegro, Serbia, and Slovenia.

Workers' self-management
The basic law for the workers' self-management entered into force in 1950, marking the end of state ownership. A system of social ownership and social workers' management of companies began.

Jadranska Magistrala
Start of the construction of the Adriatic Highway.

Socialist Federal Republic of Yugoslavia
The Federal Republic of Yugoslavia was renamed to Socialist Federal Republic of Yugoslavia.

1,900

1,950

1,940

2,159

before 1940 | 1940 | 1945 | 1950 | 1955 | 1960 | 1961 | 1962 | 1963

Tourist arrivals in Croatia
foreign tourists
domestic tourists
hotels/motels described in this travel guide

14

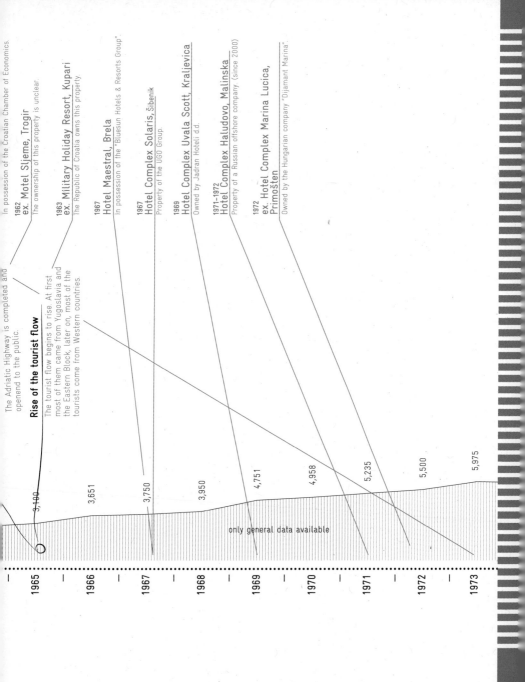

In possession of the Croatian Chamber of Economics.

1962
ex. Motel Sljeme, Trogir
The ownership of this property is unclear.

1963
ex. Military Holiday Resort, Kupari
The Republic of Croatia owns this property.

1967
Hotel Maestral, Brela
In possession of the "Bluesun Hotels & Resorts Group".

1967
Hotel Complex Solaris, Šibenik
Property of the UGO Group.

1969
Hotel Complex Uvala Scott, Kraljevica
Owned by Jadran Hoteli d.d.

1971-1972
Hotel Complex Haludovo, Malinska
Property of a Russian offshore company (since 2000)

1972
ex. Hotel Complex Marina Lucica, Primošten
Owned by the Hungarian company "Dijamant Marina".

The Adriatic Highway is completed and openend to the public.

Rise of the tourist flow

The tourist flow begins to rise. At first most of them came from Yugoslavia and the Eastern Block, later on, most of the tourists come from Western countries.

3,480

3,651

3,750

3,950

4,751

4,958

5,235

5,500

5,975

only general data available

1965 — 1966 — 1967 — 1968 — 1969 — 1970 — 1971 — 1972 — 1973

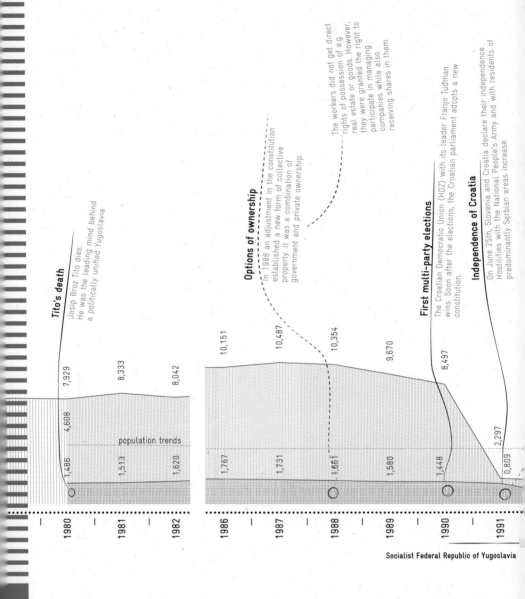

Tito's death

Josip Broz Tito dies.
He was the leading mind behind
a politically unified Yugoslavia

7,929

8,333

8,042

4,608

1,486

population trends

1,513

1,620

Options of ownership

In 1988 an adjustment in the constitution
established a new form of collective
property. It was a combination of
government and private ownership.

The workers did not get direct
rights of possession of e.g.
real estate or goods. However,
they were granted the right to
participate in managing
companies while also
receiving shares in them.

First multi-party elections

The Croatian Democratic Union (HDZ) with its leader Franjo Tudjman
wins. Soon after the elections, the Croatian parliament adopts a new
constitution.

Independence of Croatia

On June 25th, Slovenia and Croatia declare their independence
Hostilities with the National People's Army and with residents of
predominantly Serbian areas increase.

10,151

10,487

10,354

9,670

8,497

2,297

1,767

1,731

1,661

1,580

1,448

0,809

| 1980 | 1981 | 1982 | 1986 | 1987 | 1988 | 1989 | 1990 | 1991 |

Socialist Federal Republic of Yugoslavia

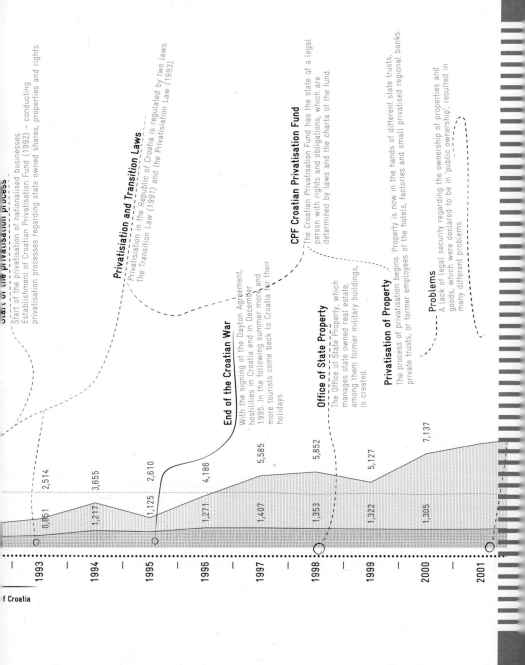

Start of the privatisation process
Start of the privatisation of nationalised businesses.
Establishment of Croatian Privatisation Fund (1992) – conducting privatisation processes regarding state owned shares, properties and rights.

Privatisation and Transition Laws
Privatisation in the Republic of Croatia is regulated by two laws.
The Transition Law (1991) and the Privatisation Law (1993).

End of the Croatian War
With the signing of the Dayton Agreement, hostilities in Croatia end in December 1995. In the following summer more and more tourists come back to Croatia for their holidays.

Office of State Property
The Office of State Property, which manages state owned real estate, among them former military buildings, is created.

Privatisation of Property
The process of privatisation begins. Property is now in the hands of different state trusts, private trusts, or former employees of the hotels, factories and small privatised regional banks.

CPF Croatian Privatisation Fund
The Croatian Privatisation Fund has the state of a legal person with rights and obligations, which are determined by laws and the charta of the fund.

Problems
A lack of legal security regarding the ownership of properties and goods, which were declared to be in 'public ownership,' resulted in many different problems.

1993	1994	1995	1996	1997	1998	1999	2000	2001

2,514   3,655   2,610   4,186   5,585   5,852   5,127   7,137

0,851   1,217   1,125   1,271   1,407   1,353   1,322   1,305

f Croatia

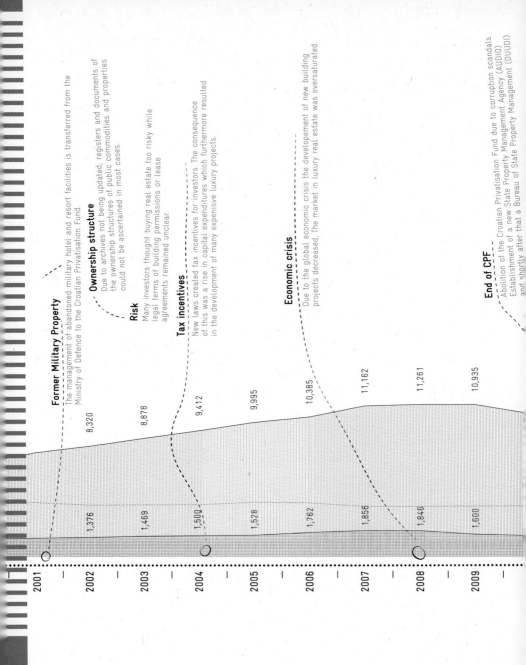

Former Military Property
The management of abandoned military hotel and resort facilities is transferred from the Ministry of Defence to the Croatian Privatisation Fund.

Ownership structure
Due to archives not being updated, registers and documents of the ownership structures of public commodities and properties could not be ascertained in most cases.

Risk
Many investors thought buying real estate too risky while legal terms of building permissions or lease agreements remained unclear.

Tax incentives
New laws created tax incentives for investors. The consequence of this was a rise in capital expenditures which furthermore resulted in the development of many expensive luxury projects.

Economic crisis
Due to the global economic crisis the developement of new building projects decreased. The market in luxury real estate was oversaturated.

End of CPF
Abolition of the Croatian Privatisation Fund due to corruption scandals. Establishment of a new State Property Management Agency (AUDIO). Establishment of a Bureau of State Property Management (DUUDI). and shortly after that a Bureau of State Property Management (DUUDI).

2001

2002   8,320   1,376

2003   8,878   1,469

2004   9,412   1,500

2005   9,995   1,528

2006   10,385   1,762

2007   11,162   1,856

2008   11,261   1,846

2009   10,935   1,600

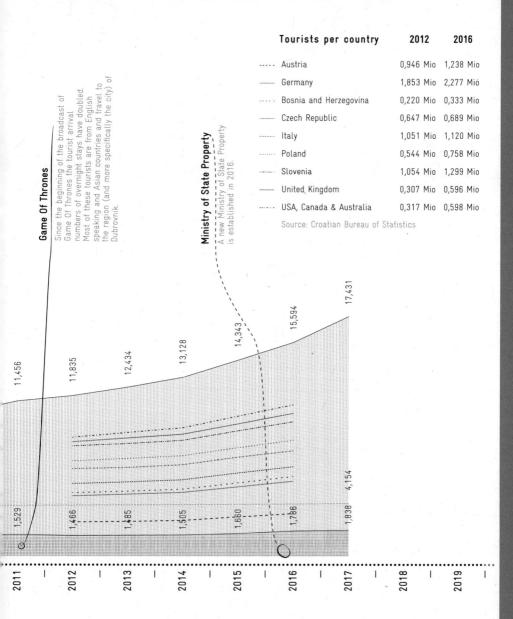

Tourists per country	2012	2016
----- Austria	0,946 Mio	1,238 Mio
——— Germany	1,853 Mio	2,277 Mio
· · · · · Bosnia and Herzegovina	0,220 Mio	0,333 Mio
········ Czech Republic	0,647 Mio	0,689 Mio
········ Italy	1,051 Mio	1,120 Mio
········ Poland	0,544 Mio	0,758 Mio
········ Slovenia	1,054 Mio	1,299 Mio
——— United Kingdom	0,307 Mio	0,596 Mio
····· USA, Canada & Australia	0,317 Mio	0,598 Mio

Source: Croatian Bureau of Statistics

Game Of Thrones

Since the beginning of the broadcast of Game Of Thrones the tourist arrival numbers of overnight stays have doubled. Most of these tourists are from English speaking and Asian countries and travel to the region (and more specifically the city) of Dubrovnik.

Ministry of State Property

A new Ministry of State Property is established in 2016.

11,456

11,835

12,434

13,128

14,343

15,594

17,431

1,529

1,466

1,485

1,505

1,660

1,786

1,838

4,154

2011 2012 2013 2014 2015 2016 2017 2018 2019

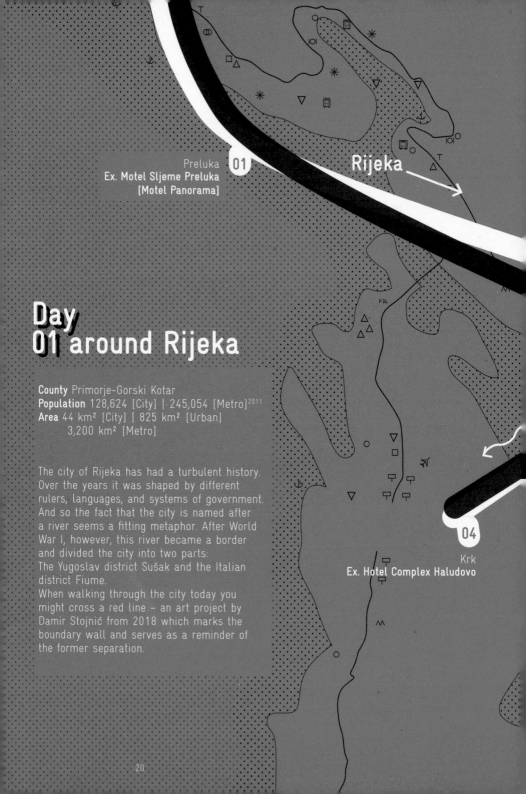

Preluka **01**
Ex. Motel Sljeme Preluka
[Motel Panorama]

Rijeka

Day
01 around Rijeka

County Primorje-Gorski Kotar
Population 128,624 [City] | 245,054 [Metro][2011]
Area 44 km² [City] | 825 km² [Urban]
    3,200 km² [Metro]

The city of Rijeka has had a turbulent history.
Over the years it was shaped by different
rulers, languages, and systems of government.
And so the fact that the city is named after
a river seems a fitting metaphor. After World
War I, however, this river became a border
and divided the city into two parts:
The Yugoslav district Sušak and the Italian
district Fiume.
When walking through the city today you
might cross a red line – an art project by
Damir Stojnić from 2018 which marks the
boundary wall and serves as a reminder of
the former separation.

Pk

04

Krk
Ex. Hotel Complex Haludovo

Rijeka
Hotel Neboder

02

03

Rijeka
Hotel Complex Uvala Scott

Krk

Did you know
That Rijeka is the European Capital of Culture
in 2020?
As a part of it, the ship "Galeb", which used
to be owned by Tito and lay vacant in the port
of Rijeka for a long time, is being converted
into a museum.

Best place to eat [fish]
In the neighbourhood of Podmurvice – not
in the city centre, but definitely worth the
journey – the tavern "Girica" offers fresh fish
from its affiliated little fish market.

Best place to go out
Nemo Pub, hidden on a traffic island between
the main road and the river Rječina, is a nice
little bar with a great atmosphere.

Don't miss
Visit the marketplace near the port, with its
impressive 100 year old fish market.

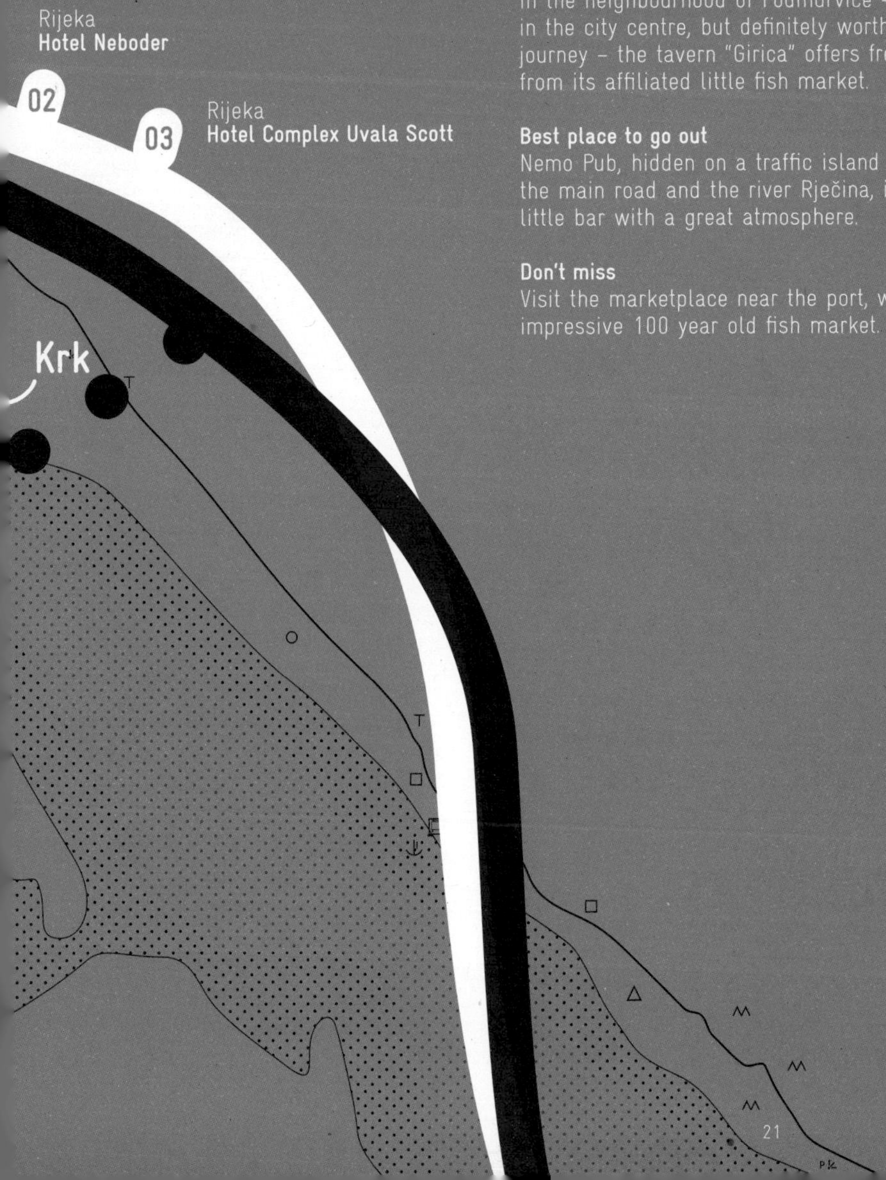

21

01

45°21'18.0"N
14°20'12.4"E
[mobile geocode] 45.355000 | 14.336778
Pavlovac ul. 2,
51000 Rijeka

ex. Motel Sljeme Preluka
[Motel Panorama]
near Rijeka

•1

Architect	Ivan Vitić
Built	1965
Renovated	–
Original Use	Motel
Current Use	vacant
Distribution of property	owned by the Croatian Chamber of Commerce
Good to know	listed as cultural heritage since 2015; winner of the "Borba" Federal Award for Architecture for the best architectural work of Croatia and Yugoslavia in 1965

The motel in Preluka near Rijeka, also known as Motel Panorama, is part of a motel chain Ivan Vitić planned for the agricultural industrial combine Sljeme. Three out of five originally planned motels were built, in Preluka, Biograd na Moru and Trogir. In all cases, Vitić designed the functionality and shaped visual connections corresponding to the perspective of a car driver, while also showing a sensitive approach to the different topographical situations. For the special hillside location in Preluka, he used a linear system which only opens up gradually after you enter the complex. Another characteristic of Vitić's motel chain is the cladding of the outer walls and interior public areas with stones from local quarries.

Since 1996, the motel in Preluka has been owned by the Croatian Chamber of Commerce and has stood vacant for many years. In 2015, thanks to the initiative "Motel Trogir", it was listed as cultural heritage. However, because its buildung physics would demand substantial changes to bring it up to date, the question of what is to be done with the object is still unresolved.

photo Bernadette Krejs

02

Hotel Neboder
Rijeka

•2

Architect	Josip Pičman, Alfred Albini
Built	1935–1947
Renovated	2007
Original Use	Hotel
Current Use	Hotel
Distribution of property	owned by the hotel group Jadran hoteli d.d. Rijeka
Good to know	The hotel tower is one floor higher than the second high-rise building of Rijeka.

The Hotel Neboder (Croatian for "skyscraper") is part of the HKD cultural centre in Rijeka, built between 1935 and 1947. Due to various aggravating circumstances, the construction took more than 10 years. The project, which Josip Pičman designed for a competition, was finally built by Alfred Albini with some modifications and cost-saving measures. It was built during the inter-war period when Rijeka was divided between Italy and the Kingdom of Yugoslavia – and thus the fourteen-storey hotel tower was in direct competition with the high-rise in the Italian sector built in 1939–1942. In the 1960s, the café on the top floor of the Hotel Neboder was a popular meeting place for Rijeka's local population. Today, the offices of the hotel group Jadran hoteli, which also manages the hotel, are located there. Hotel Neboder was slightly renovated in 2007, but currently there are plans for a larger refurbishment to increase the classification from three to four stars.

03

Hotel Complex Uvala Scott
Kraljevica, Dubno Bay

•3

Architect	Igor Emili
Built	1968
Renovated	-
Original Use	Hotel
Current Use	Hotel
Distribution of property	owned by the hotel group Jadran hoteli d.d. Rijeka
Good to know	The hotel remains mostly unchanged except for a few maintenance measures. Most of the interior design also dates back to the time of its establishment.

Uvala Scott is a hotel complex consisting of a main building and 11 pavilions. It is located in a bay, not far from the town of Kraljevica and next to the bridge to the island of Krk. In the 1960s the architect Igor Emili was commissioned to plan a hotel on the site, which in the 19th century was owned by the Englishman Alexander Scott. The new hotel was opened in 1968.

Emili designed the hotel as a city. The core of the hotel complex consisted of narrow streets, arcades and terraces. Emili incorporated the historical structures of the site into his design and combined them with the authentic character of the environment. This was a new approach in the context of tourism developments in post-war modernism, and it was celebrated by critics under the name of critical regionalism. The existing buildings from the time of Alexander Scott were integrated into the project: The old family house was turned into a restaurant, the stables into a disco-club and the fisherman's hut into a tavern. These venues and especially the night-club, attracted many young people from Rijeka and the surrounding area until the 1990s. The hotel is still operating.

photo Jadran hoteli d.d. Rijeka

04

ex. Hotel Complex Haludovo
Malinska, Krk Island

Architect	Boris Magaš
Built	1969–1972
Renovated	–
Original Use	Hotel complex
Current Use	partially used as hotel, most parts vacant
Distribution of property	Since the privatisation of the complex in the 1990s, different companies with different company locations alternate; since the 2000s, the Russian-Armenian entrepreneur Ara Abramyan appears as majority owner.
Good to know	Decades of dispute between the municipality of Malinska and the owner regarding the privatisation of the coastal zone.

photos Maria Groiss

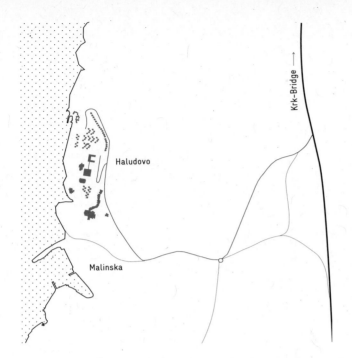

45°07'51.0"N
14°31'40.4"E

45.130833 | 14.527889

51511 Malinska, Krk

The hotel complex Haludovo, north of Malinska on the island of Krk, is an ensemble of various architectural typologies. The resort consisted of a central building – the Hotel Palace, the neighbouring Hotel Tamaris, two clusters of atrium-bungalows, a beach bar, a chain of two-storey apartment houses, a detached reception building and a "fishermen's village" including a small port. The style of the individual buildings varies from modern to postmodern, and can be read as the beginning of new tendencies in the region's tourism architecture. The complex was designed by the architect Boris Magaš and built from 1969 to 1972 on behalf of the state-owned trading company Brodokomerc. Shortly after the opening, Penthouse magazine publisher Bob Guccione took over the resort and turned it into the "Penthouse Adriatic Club". The spacious lobby was converted into a casino and so-called "penthouse pets" worked there as hostesses and croupiers. The Penthouse-Brodokomerc partnership didn't last long, but the resort remained a hotspot for upper class guests. Nevertheless, the entire area with its landscape carefully designed by Magaš and his team remained open to the public. In particular, the beach zone with its specially designed lounging nooks is still popular among the local population.

During the Yugoslav Wars in the 1990s, the complex was used as a shelter for refugees. In the 2000s, it was bought by a Russian-Armenian offshore company based in Cyprus. Since 2002, the majority of the complex has been vacant. Only a very small part is in use today: the postmodern "fishermen's village", as well as the two-storey apartment buildings lined up along the access road.

Today, the ruin of Haludovo is probably the most famous and most photographed "Lost Place" in Croatia, attracting both urban explorers and curious tourists.

photo Lucia de la Duena Sotelo

Timeline
of hotel
complex
Haludovo

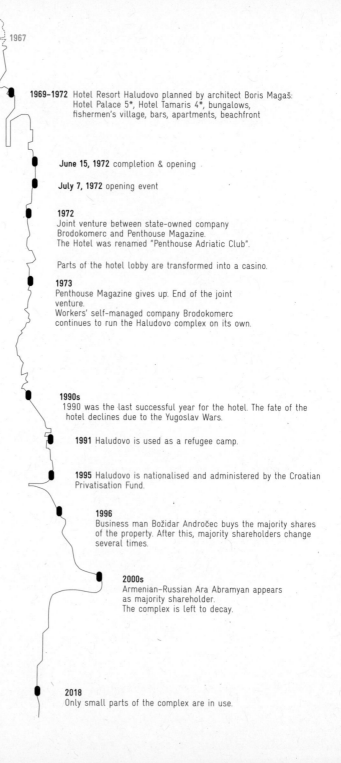

1967

1969–1972 Hotel Resort Haludovo planned by architect Boris Magaš:
Hotel Palace 5*, Hotel Tamaris 4*, bungalows,
fishermen's village, bars, apartments, beachfront

June 15, 1972 completion & opening .

July 7, 1972 opening event

1972
Joint venture between state-owned company
Brodokomerc and Penthouse Magazine.
The Hotel was renamed "Penthouse Adriatic Club".

Parts of the hotel lobby are transformed into a casino.

1973
Penthouse Magazine gives up. End of the joint
venture.
Workers' self-managed company Brodokomerc
continues to run the Haludovo complex on its own.

1990s
1990 was the last successful year for the hotel. The fate of the
hotel declines due to the Yugoslav Wars.

1991 Haludovo is used as a refugee camp.

1995 Haludovo is nationalised and administered by the Croatian
Privatisation Fund.

1996
Business man Božidar Andročec buys the majority shares
of the property. After this, majority shareholders change
several times.

2000s
Armenian–Russian Ara Abramyan appears
as majority shareholder.
The complex is left to decay.

2018
Only small parts of the complex are in use.

Haludovo Site

•4

•5

Adriatic Sea

1 Reception
2 Hotel Palace
3 Hotel Tamaris
4 Beach Bar & Restaurant
5 Fishermen's Village
6 Atrium Bungalows
7 Apartments

● in use
● abandoned | vacant

Hotel Palace
1968–72

A swimming pool [outdoor]
B swimming pool [indoor]
C hall
D lobby
E rooms
F pergola
G beach promenade

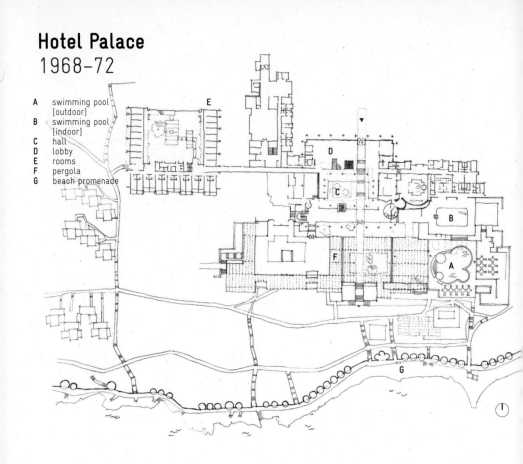

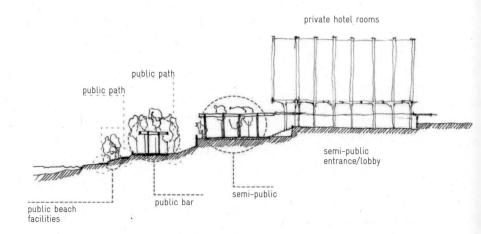

private hotel rooms

public path

public path

semi-public
entrance/lobby

public beach
facilities

public bar

semi-public

Bungalows
1968–80

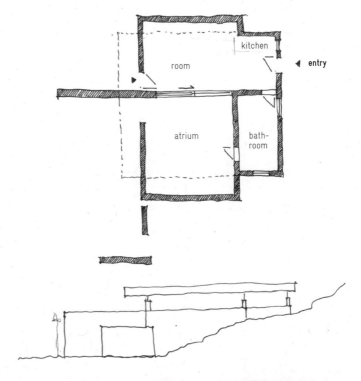

photo Antonia Dika

photo Maria Groiss

"These hotels were anything but modest. They provided high standards, glamorous interior design, and explicitly modern artwork commisssioned from the nation's most acclaimed contemporary artists."

Michael Zinganel
From "Social Tourism" to a Mass Market Consumer Paradise, p. 50–53.

Adriatic Coast Between Mass Tourism and Cold War

Antonia Dika

Antonia Dika
is a Vienna-based architect, urban planner and researcher. She was born in Rijeka, studied architecture in Vienna and Berlin and currently holds the position of senior scientist at the University of Art and Design Linz. From 2009 to 2018, she worked for the City of Vienna's Urban Renewal Office (GB*7/8/16). Since 2007, Dika investigates Cold War military facilities on Adriatic islands and currently leads the research project "Collective Utopias of Post-War Modernism: the Adriatic Coast as a Leisure and Defence Paradise" funded by the Austrian Science Fund.

[1]
Igor Tschoukarine, "The Yugoslav Road to International Tourism," in Yugoslavia's Sunny Side: A History of Tourism in Socialism (1950s–1980s), eds. Hannes Grandits and Karin Taylor (Budapest and New York: CEU Press, 2010), 107–138.

[2]
Therefore, it is not easy to make any statements regarding the foundation years, military strategies etc. today. Many years of military secrecy and the war which followed, splitting the military into opposing sides, have left huge gaps in the archives.

One of the first slogans used in the aftermath of World War II to entice tourists to visit the Socialist Federal Republic of Yugoslavia was "Come and see the Truth" [1]. The truth that was to be seen here meant the success of Tito's Third Way and socialist self-government. Visitors coming from both East and West were supposed to personally convince themselves of the progress achieved by this non-aligned country. A progress which was also to be reflected in the innovative architecture of its hotels and tourist facilities spreading along its 6,000 kilometres of coastline. Thanks to the unprecedented and never since repeated construction programmes, this so far predominantly rural area underwent rapid touristic urbanisation in just a few years. At the same time, along the very same coastal area, yet hidden from the eyes of the public, a different kind of construction programme was implemented to a similar extent, only this time for military purposes. Yugoslavia, as a non-aligned country, wedged between the NATO in the West and the Warsaw Pact in the East, had to secure its borders against both. The western border towards Italy ran almost entirely along the sea, turning the coast with its many offshore islands into the first line of defence.

The establishment of military bases started shortly after the war; they were extended and developed until the 1980s. Planning and construction were carried out in strict secrecy. The bases were not recorded in any official documents such as maps, zoning plans or land registers. [2] On the other hand, the media and the general public followed the touristic urbanisation with great interest. In 1963, the Yugoslav government asked the United Nations for assistance with regard to the elaboration of strategic development plans for the coastal region. Besides tourist facilities, these plans also included industrial sites, since it was held that a mono-functional economy relying only on tourism couldn't successfully function, even on the coast. This resulted in spatial development plans called "Adriatic Projects" (Jadranski projekti) that were developed by Yugoslav and international experts, including planners from NATO member states such as the United Kingdom, France, or Italy. [3] A paradoxical situation arose in which the experts from countries representing a potential threat were hired to develop urbanisation strategies for areas in which (secret) military posts for protection against their own countries were established.

It is hard to answer with certainty whether the international UN planners and developers were aware of the fact that alongside tourism and industry, the military was also competing for the very same coastal area. In any case, the "Adriatic Projects" do not reveal any type of military presence, and some hatchings marking tourist areas actually overlap with prohibited military zones. [4]
Such examples can be found on the islands of Vis and Lastovo, where foreign citizens were completely denied access for military security reasons, and international tourism was not able to gain a foothold until the ban was lifted in 1988. In some other places, however, tourist hotspots were developed in immediate proximity to military exclusion zones, despite top secret policies. This was the case for example on the island of Lošinj and near Zadar, where the military site Šepurine was located next to the tourist resort Punta Skala. Reflecting the zeitgeist of the Cold War era, miles of barbed wire fences along tourist access roads or warships at anchor in civilian harbours apparently did not seem unusual, neither to the local population nor to foreign visitors. [5]

Behind the barbed wire fence the scenery was mostly the same: on sites facing the open sea, especially on the outer islands, cannon systems were positioned to prevent potential invasion by foreign vessels. Some posts also included missile defence systems. They were surrounded by their associated military camps used for the accommodation of soldiers. Depending on their size, some of them were equipped with training areas, workshops, parade grounds or clinics; favourably situated bays were used as military harbours including (underground) ammunition depots and fuel tanks. Additionally, a number of ship bunkers were distributed along the coast and on the islands. Whether in the case of simple army barracks that imitated local residential homes, or in the case of "invisible" bunker facilities, their architecture was generally standardised and only adapted slightly to accommodate the geographical features of different locations. An exception were facilities with a primarily representative function which were not shrouded in the veil of military secrecy: "Dom JNA"-buildings (literally translated: "homes of the Yugoslav People's Army"), something like cultural centres managed by the army, serving as an interface between military staff and the local population. They mostly included dining facilities and hosted concerts, film screenings, dance performances, chess tournaments or even weddings. The prices there were lower than in comparable civilian or commercial establishments. Especially in smaller municipalities, for instance on the islands, these types of venues played an important role in the cultural life of the community. They were situated in prominent locations and their representative character was also reflected in their architecture. As in the case of the tourist facilities of this period, Dom JNA buildings served as a testing ground for the

[3]
Vladimir Mattioni, Jadranski Projekti (Zagreb: Urbanistički institut Hrvatske, 2003), 8–15.

[4]
However, the "Adriatic Projects" were rarely implemented in real life, mostly due to the fact that they were finalised when touristic urbanisation was already progressing at full pace.

[5]
A number of people interviewed on the island of Mali Lošinj emphasised that strong military presence was completely normal to them, and that they only started to think about it after the outbreak of the war in Yugoslavia. (According to interviews carried out in August 2018 by Antonia Dika and Anamarija Batista as part of the project "Collective Utopias of Post-War Modernism: The Adriatic Coast as a Leisure and Defence Paradise").

[6]
Interview with Darko Lendić, former receptionist at the Krvavica military resort, in Nikolina Džeko, "Rikard Marasovićs Kindersanatorium in Krvavica. Bestandsaufnahme und Revitalisierung" (Diploma thesis, TU Vienna, 2014), 86.

[7]
Ahmet Kalajdžić, "Kupari nižu uspjehe", Slobodna Dalmacija, December 22, 1989, 18.

[8]
The coastline was defined as common property to which every citizen must have access at all times. Even in today's Croatia, privatisation of "maritime property" is prohibited, but concessions up to 99 years can be sought.

[9]
Many military facilities played their role in the Yugoslav War, but less because of their strategic positions than for their equipment and staff.

[10]
Despite various announcements, no former military space has been transformed into a tourist resort so far. In contrast to the Croatian experience, the military barracks "Orjenski Bataljon" in Kumbor, Montenegro, recently were converted into the Portonovi Montenegro luxury resort.

[11]
The difficulty of repurposing such (long-standing) state-owned real estate also becomes visible when looking at the numerous offices, funds, agencies and sub-agencies that have managed them since the 1990s and whose competences partially overlapped. In 2016, even a "Ministry of State Property" was established.

best architects of the country. Ivan Vitić, the designer of the award-winning motel chain Sljeme, created three exceptional buildings for the National Army: Dom JNA Komiža (on the island of Vis), Dom JNA Split and Dom JNA Šibenik.

Another type of military architecture that was not subject to military secrecy included military facilities built for tourism. Like many other organisations in socialist Yugoslavia, the Army also managed its own holiday resorts in the spirit of the idea of "social tourism". Here, military staff had the opportunity to spend holidays with their families at a low cost — with guests ranging from high-ranking officers to cleaning personnel, which is why accommodation standards and architectural quality differed among the facilities. When not booked to full capacity, they were also open to external guests. Some facilities even accepted international tourists, albeit under different terms. [6] The Kupari military holiday resort was highly appreciated in the 1980s among foreign tourists, even though they were only able to book in low season, since the high season was fully booked by military staff. [7] The public and semi-public areas of such facilities, including the beach areas were freely accessible for everyone, which was the case for all tourist facilities of socialist Yugoslavia. [8]

The majority of post-war military structures, as well as many tourist facilities, remain vacant today. In both cases, they have lost their original function after the outbreak of the Yugoslav Wars: the tourist facilities due to the lack of tourists, and the military ones due to their wrong orientation. [9] Just like the majority of hotels, some military barracks were also used for the accommodation of refugees during and after the war. While the privatisation of tourist facilities had already started during the war with different types of ownership models, the Croatian military kept the facilities "inherited" from the JNA for itself. But gradually they were declared to "lack prospects" and were given up, although in most cases the Republic of Croatia is still listed as their official owner. Various "utilisation plans" developed by different governments, which usually envisaged their transformation into luxurious tourist resorts by major foreign investors, have failed so far. [10] Years have passed, laws and authorities have changed. [11] Even though the buildings are state-owned, most of the facilities are implicated in land tenure issues that still need to be resolved. Constantly changing construction laws and unconfirmed zoning plans additionally hamper ambitions for their conversion. The facilities situated within cities were a bit better placed in this regard, as some of them are being repurposed for civilian use. However, most of the former military facilities, built to protect the south-western border of Yugoslavia, were situated outside urban centres, and in many cases on small, remote islands with few inhabitants.

While some post-war tourist facilities have successfully returned
to their original function, there have only been a few, if remarkable
examples of repurposing former military structures: On the island
of Vis, a wine cellar was integrated into a former power supply bunker,
and on the island of Lastovo, a car mechanic now operates within an
ex-military warehouse. The training pitch of the local football club
of Vis used to be the parade ground of the Samogor military barracks,
which were temporarily repurposed for various workshops, art and
architecture camps in the previous years. Other military barracks
on the island of Vis were temporarily turned into horse stables.
On the island of Korčula, a former military building now hosts the
municipal olive oil mill. These small-scale examples of (not always
legal) repurposing, implemented with limited funds on the local level,
demonstrate the many creative uses of existing resources, which
can ideally be beneficial to the whole community. They also
demonstrate that what is lacking is not ideas or "visions". Even if they
are certainly not the only and also not the "most profitable" options
for dealing with the heritage of post-war construction programmes,
they serve as a reminder that things can be achieved without waiting
for large investors.

<<
View from a former military observation
tower on the Island of Vis.
Photo Daniele Ansidei, 2007.

Day
02 around Zadar

County Zadar
Population 75,082 [City] [2011]
Area 194 km² [City]

Zadar is one of the oldest cities of Croatia.
The historic city is located on a narrow
headland, apart from the new town. Until
1873, the city was a fortress. A walk
through the old town seems like a journey
through time: from ruins of Roman buildings,
ancient city walls and medieval gates to
modern architecture and contemporary art
installations. Zadar was subjected to heavy
bombing during World War II, leaving huge
gaps in the old city. In the 1950s, many of
the new buidings were designed by leading
Modernist architects, which had a lasting
impact on the cityscape.

Did you know
That Alfred Hitchcock once said: "Zadar
has the most beautiful sunset in the world,
more beautiful than the one in Key West, in
Florida, applauded at every evening."

Where to stay
Zadar's Boutique Hostel Forum is an
adaptation of a modernist block right in the
city centre. It was designed by Studio Up
and Damir Gamulin in 2013.

Don't miss
The unique sound art installation Morske
Orgulje ("Sea Organ") by architect Nikola
Bašić.

Šepurine
Ex. Military Complex

05

Zadar

05

ex. Military Complex Šepurine
Šepurine, near Zadar

Architect	unknown
Built	1950s /1960s
Renovated	The complex was renovated by the Croatian military in the 1990s adding an airfield.
Original Use	Military facility of the Yugoslav People's Army, later taken over by the Croatian military.
Current Use	various informal uses
Distribution of property	Property disputes, officially owned by the Republic of Croatia, managed by the Ministry of State Property.
Good to know	The abandoned military facility is located between two highly frequented tourist resorts: Falkensteiner Hotels & Residences Punta Skala and Zaton Holiday Resort.

photo Michaela Fodor

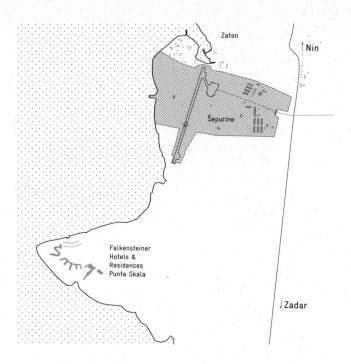

**44°12'42.1"N
15°09'41.1"E**
45.211694 | 15.16147
Šepurine,
[12 km from Zadar],
23232 Zaton

The former military facility Šepurine is located between the villages of Zaton and Petrčane, only a few minutes from the city of Zadar. It is a wide area with an abandoned 1-km-long airstrip, a mooring, some isolated barracks and workshops. All buildings are in a ruinous condition and mostly nothing but the foundations remain.

Originally, the barracks and parade ground were built by the Yugoslav People's Army in previously unspoilt nature by the sea. It became a top secret high-security zone protected by barbed wire fencing. Making it even more interesting, a short time later the tourism complex Punta Skala (now Falkensteiner Hotels & Residences) was built directly next to it, which was to attract tourists from all over the world.

During the Yugoslav Wars of the 1990s, the Croatian military took over the Šepurine complex and added a military airfield. But soon after the war, the facility was abandoned and has been left to decay ever since. In the development plan of the city of Nin, this area is designated as a tourist zone. However, unresolved ownership issues frustrated all intentions to reuse the area. Since its abandonment, the site has been the venue for various informal uses. It was used as a paintball facility, a terrain for orienteering races, a bee farm, or until recently as a car/motorcycle race track. In 2018, this was prevented by heaps of rubble on the airfield: the Ministry of State Property had authorised the Municipality of Nin to use the site as a dump for building materials.

photo Lucia de la Duena Sotelo

Timeline of Šepurine Military complex

Traces of reuse

Nov. 2017
Motor Extreme CC

rubbish dump

seaside resort

baby pool

dog & visitors path

dump depots
to limit motor
races

view to Falkensteiner resort Punta Skala

Šepurine Site

Zaton

4 min.

22 min.

Zadar

From "Social Tourism" to a Mass Market Consumer Paradise

Michael Zinganel

Michael Zinganel
studied Architecture at
Graz University of
Technology, Fine Art at the
Jan van Eyck Academy
Maastricht, and obtained
a PhD in contemporary
history at the University of
Vienna. He taught at various
universities and academies,
e.g. at the postgraduate
academy of Bauhaus
Dessau Foundation and
the TU Vienna. In 2012 he
co-founded the independent
research institute Tracing
Spaces, also co-editing
Holiday after the Fall –
Seaside Architecture and
Urbanism in Bulgaria and
Croatia with E. Beyer and
A. Hagemann,
Berlin: jovis 2013.
2014–16, he was research
associate at the Academy
of Fine Arts Vienna.

Established tourism infrastructures and architectures existed on the Croatian Adriatic before Tito's days, too. When the SFYR was established in 1945, the private hotels, grand restaurants, magnificent villas, transport companies and travel agencies established during the Austro-Hungarian Monarchy and the Yugoslav Kingdom were nationalised and subsequently merged to form new large "socialised" enterprises under "workers' self-management".

Clearly, doing whatever it took to ensure the domestic population was able go to the seaside was a greater priority for the new socialist government in Yugoslavia than opening up the country to foreigners – at least according to its rhetoric in its early years in power. First a system of "social tourism" was established both on existing nationalised sites built in the era of the monarchies, but also in new purpose-built facilities. An extensive network of holiday homes and camps was established, each of which was reserved for the staff and/ or members of one particular trade union, state administrative unit, youth organization, large "socialized company", or for the Yugoslav National Army. Domestic tourism here was also considered to be a tool for nation-building and reconciliation, enabling the population to discover and learn to respect the different cultures of their brothers (and sisters) in the multi-ethnic Federation.

According to architecture critic Maroje Mrduljaš, the first "new" type of tourist resort (odmarališta), originally introduced for social tourism purposes, perfectly illustrates the architectural and social vision of "socialist leisure": modest small single-storey pavilions designed as guest accommodation units clustered around a social centre (Društveni dom) – a comparably large central building housing a restaurant and other communal facilities for social encounter, such as a multifunctional hall, a library, billiard and chess rooms, etc. [1] The design of early commercial resorts was no different: pure camping sites with pre-fabricated pavilions, which became increasingly larger, more solidly built and more comfortably equipped, while the semi-public buildings became more diversified to offer a broader range of services and entertainment (shops, restaurants, grills, open air dance floors, indoor nightclubs etc.). Until today, similar modest facilities are typical and fundamental elements of the Croatian coastal tourism

[1]
Maroje Mrduljaš, "Building
the Affordable Arcadia.
Tourism development on
the Croatian Adriatic coast
under state socialism," in
Holidays after the Fall, eds.
Elke Beyer, Anke Hagemann,
Michael Zinganel (Berlin:
Jovis, 2013), 117.

landscape – and they are appreciated acclaimed by many tourists, because they were placed in an elaborately landscaped setting while guaranteeing unconditional free access to the seaside for all.

The first newly built motels and hotels were horizontal low-rise blocks in a sober modern design language, elevated on pillars, often consisting of several wings, some arranged around courtyards in atrium style, or in clusters discreetly dotted around the pine forests. The individual private rooms remained rather small and modest, while the design dimensions of social meeting places were comparatively "luxurious".

But Yugoslavia's cosmopolitanism also called for luxurious conference hotels at the coastline to show off international celebrities, international politicians and the movie stars, hired by Yugoslavia's booming film industry. So in the mid-1960s, following international trends, a handful of solitary high-rise hotels were built near the coastline, often at the edge of ancient towns (e.g. Neven Šegvić: Hotel Excelsior, Dubrovnik, 1965; Zdravko Bregovac: Hotel Ambasador, Opatija, 1966). These hotels were anything but modest. They provided high standards, glamorous interior design, and explicitly modern artwork commisssioned from the nation's most acclaimed contemporary artists. [2], a policy to be continued for most of the new hotels on the Adriatic coast. Not only the style and amenities of these hotels, but also the curatorial practices were inspired by the US-based hotel chain Hilton International [3]: between Communism and the American Way of Life, international guests were invited to enjoy the alternative fruits of Yugoslavia's Third Way.

The increasing demand for much higher capacities by the end of the 1960s led the solitary vertical slab or block being abandoned in favour of architectural models considered to be more compatible with the landscape. The challenge of designing large-capacity hotels, namely combining enormous inter-connected volumes for public services and backstage zones with a large number of very small private accommodation units, called for a more dynamic organisation. Large volumes therefore were deconstructed and rearranged in new forms: clusters of smaller units reproducing the imagery of a Mediterranean village (Igor Emili: Hotel Uvala Scott, Kraljevica, 1966–69), or combining several atrium or courtyard typologies to a larger but seemingly lightweight ensembles (Boris Magaš: Hotel Complex Solaris, Šibenik, 1967–68). On the Croatian Adriatic, Yugoslav architects and construction companies urged to find individual solutions for both gentle coastlines and unwieldy sloping sites. The most outstanding achievement at the Croatian Coast was the mix of different building types and the remarkable expertise in the use of sliding formworks for cast-in-situ concrete to realise spectacular structuralist formations

[2]
Even a "visual arts supervisor" was commissioned, namely Boris Vižintin, then director of the Gallery of Modern Art in Rijeka. See: Mrduljaš, "Building the Affordable Arcadia," 201.

[3]
Built at the time of the expansion of the political influence of the USA, these hotels were considered to promote an American Lifestyle and the "fruits of the free world" at strategically important destinations. See Annabel Jane Wharton, Building the Cold War: Hilton International Hotels and Modern Architecture (Chicago: University of Chicago Press, 2001).

[4]
Interview with Boris Magaš, Croatian architect of the famous resorts Solaris in Šibenik and Haludovo in Malinska/Krk, Kraljevica (August 24, 2012).

in exposed concrete – despite rather limited financial resources: for instance, staggered complexes expanding as multi-layered architectural landscapes in the flat slopes of Istrian pine forests (Julije De Luca: Brulo, Poreč, 1970) or terraced volumes skilfully embedded in the Dalmatian coast's rugged rock formations (Andrija Čičin-Šain, Žarko Vincek, Hotel Libertas in Dubrovnik, 1970).

For the architects involved in Croatia as well as in other coastal destinations, the rise of the tourism industry represented a very welcome opportunity for spatial experiments, but also for transgressing the Modernist self-limitation to purely rational and functional design [4]: tourism architecture stages both the landscape and the people, while also becoming part of the landscape. At its best, tourist architecture is as modern as the tourist practice and the beach experience itself, yet simultaneously reveals a destination's special qualities, and respects the tourist's longing for an exceptional and/ or even romantic experience. Therefore, it calls for regional references, the integration of local building traditions and materials, and the implementation of a more expressive and emotional design language. Architecture guides tourists' feet as well as their gazes along the most attractive sights and sites of the tourist landscape.

Architects brilliantly understood and supported these longings: plants penetrated from the surrounding landscape into the often terraced semi-public spaces, lobbies, dining rooms, staircases, and also the rooms' balconies. On entering the lobby, guests immediately enjoyed a framed image of the seaside's horizon, the silhouette of a Venetian village on a peninsula at a distance. In the best case the sun would even set behind its campanile. Harbour towns and fishermen's villages were interconnected by seaside promenades passing through pine forests. Dance floors placed near pools used the vivid light reflections of the water to enhance the atmosphere.
Yugoslavia's coastline was an affordable arcadia for feeling "modern" – an honest and affordable paradise for those western European tourists who didn't chase after the higher status of more prestigious travel destinations.

Instead of a peaceful transformation from Yugoslavia's Third Way economy to pure market capitalism, the Federation was shattered by nationalist aspirations, and years of warfare and ethnic cleansing, starting during the summer season of 1991. A few hotels suffered from attacks during the war, but – more importantly – 80 percent of them were used to accommodate war refugees, many staying for several years.

Architects admiring the Socialist Modernist buildings, in former Yugoslavia and abroad, had feared that this heritage would be in danger of demolition and reconstruction because of anti-socialist resentment and the expected neoliberal building boom following the war. Interestingly – until Croatia's EU accession in 2013 – melancholy vacant hotels and resort ruins still outnumbered significant new developments. The many years of war, disinvestment, and a long, drawn-out and intransparent privatisation process radically delayed the introduction of investment-friendly policies. This was caused by high debts of businesses and complex ownership structures, chauvinism and corruption, conspiracies with supporters, and a lack of legal security regarding land and property ownership, which before had been socially owned by all Yugoslavs. Ironically, in Croatia "liberalism" started in 1991 with the nationalisation of all socially-owned property and self-managed businesses, later to be delivered into the private hands of "good patriots" and government cronies.

But often new owners of large tourism enterprises suffered from the distrust of local stakeholders. Nevertheless, it was possible to re-establish awareness for the value of the modernist heritage, with major construction projects becoming subject to strict building regulations. A few years after the first large reinvestments had begun, the economy was again badly hit by the global economic crisis of 2008–2011.

From another point of view, this development, justly criticised as mismanagement and maladministration by liberal economists and leftists alike, can be interpreted as a historically lucky twist of fate: in contrast to the disastrous disfiguration of the coastlines of Spain, Bulgaria, or Montenegro, Croatia's natural resources and landscape have largely been kept intact. And many of the ruins and unrenovated buildings serve as perfect 1:1 museums of Modernist design ideas – obviously attracting new groups of visitors.

>>
President Tito looking at the model of the planned Adriatic II conference hotel in Opatija, ca. 1971. Source: Archive of Hrvatski Muzej Turizma Opatija.

Handwritten on the back of the photo: "President Tito observing the model of the Adriatic Hotel II and the congress hall that was opened on May 25, 1971 with the FIS Congress attended by delegates from 42 countries.

Šibenik
Hotel Complex Solaris **08**

Šibenik
Ex. Hall of the Yugoslav
People's Army [Dom JNA]
06

Šibenik

Day
03 around Šibenik

County Šibenik-Knin
Population 34,302 [City] | 46,332 [Metro] [2011]
Area 404 km² [City] | 433 km² [Metro]

While in the newer districts to the north
and northeast of Šibenik there are many
newly built holiday homes, the centre has
a well-protected medieval heart where you
will find numerous churches, monasteries
and palaces – the cultural heritage of an
important history. You may wander through
the stone labyrinth of steep backstreets and
alleys – assuming you aren't short of breath,
because Šibenik is a city of stairs. Only a
narrow channel connects Šibenik to the sea.
But when you take a boat or ferry through
the narrow estuary mouth into the open sea,
you will discover a variety of beautiful small
islands, for instance the island of Zlarin.

Zlarin

Zlarin Island
Ex. Military Complex Zlarin **07**

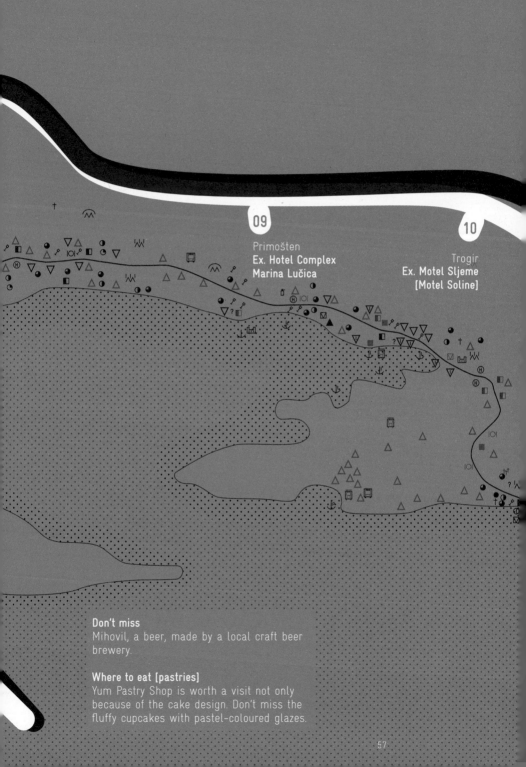

09

Primošten
Ex. Hotel Complex
Marina Lučica

10

Trogir
Ex. Motel Sljeme
[Motel Soline]

Don't miss
Mihovil, a beer, made by a local craft beer
brewery.

Where to eat [pastries]
Yum Pastry Shop is worth a visit not only
because of the cake design. Don't miss the
fluffy cupcakes with pastel-coloured glazes.

06

43°44'04.1"N
15°53'35.0"E
43.734457 | 15.893052
Poljana 6,
22000 Šibenik

Ex. Hall of the Yugoslav People's Army
[Dom JNA]
Šibenik

•6

Architect	Ivan Vitić
Built	1961
Renovated	2005
Original Use	Hall of the Yugoslav People's Army, cultural centre run by the military
Current Use	City library "Juraj Šižgorić"
Distribution of property	City of Šibenik
Good to know	Located in the historic centre, the new modern building was quite heavily criticised at the time of its creation.

Dom JNA, literally meaning "Yugoslav People's Army Home", was a cultural centre run by the military. In each town with a larger military presence, a Dom JNA was established. It was a representative space for the army where the civilian population and the military could "informally" come together. Concerts, exhibitions, film screenings or theatre plays, dance events or other shows took place there. The Dom JNA building complex in Šibenik, which also included a primary school, was designed by the architect Ivan Vitić (from Šibenik himself) in 1961. Situated on the edge of the historic Gothic-Renaissance city, Vitić's design integrated the old city walls into the building. The construction of the folded roof acts as a load-bearing component, allowing spacious halls in the interior with only a few delicate pillars, as well as large glass facades. After it's abandonment by the army, it was turned into a City Library in 2005. It was one of the first official transformations of former military buildings for civilian purposes. Since its renovation, the initial spaciousness of the interior can no longer be fully experienced, because of an additional gallery level added for library purposes.

photo Cristina Krois

07

Ex. Military Complex Zlarin
Zlarin Island

Architect	unknown
Built	first interventions already in the Austro-Hungarian era, expansion of the complex by the JNA after World War II
Original Use	Military complex with cannon positions
Current Use	vacant
Distribution of property	Republic of Croatia, Administration by Ministry of State Property
Good to know	Artists Tonka Maleković and Lina Rica used the facility for an art installation in 2008.

photo Antonia Dika

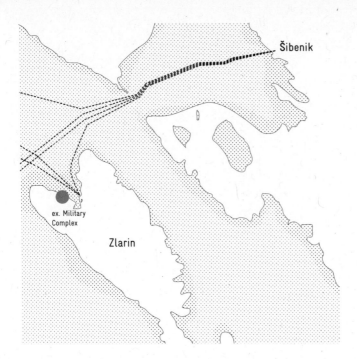

43°42'01.9"N
15°49'27.2"E
43.700528 | 15.824222
22232, Zlarin,
Šibenik

Šibenik

ex. Military
Complex

Zlarin

The tiny island of Zlarin with its 8 km² and currently 276 registered inhabitants was an important part of the military defences of Šibenik during the time of the Austro-Hungarian Monarchy. After the World War II, the Yugoslav People's Army expanded the existing cannon positions at Cap Marin with a military barracks complex. Like many other military facilities along the islands and the coast, it was abandoned in the 1990s. In the following years, it was often used for informal camping by excursionists from neighbouring coastal towns.
In 2008, artists Tonka Maleković and Lina Rica used the facility for an art installation, traces of which are still visible. In 2014, a heavy thunderstorm devastated the already battered barracks buildings. In the current land use plan, the area is designated as a tourist zone.

Legend

01 military barracks, ruins

02 mole

03 beach

04 path

05 underground bunker (5-6 rooms)

06 defensive walls

07 large rocks and stones

08 gate (removed)

photos Cristina Krois, Philip Langer, Sarah Gold

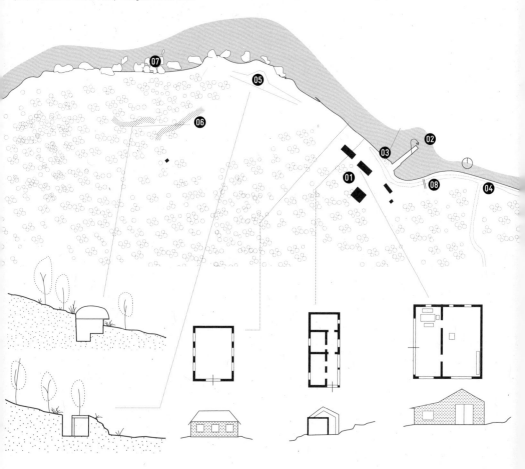

08

Solaris Hotel Complex
Šibenik

•7

Architect	Boris Magaš
Built	1967 / 1969 / 1972
Renovated	several renovations and alterations over the years
Original Use	Hotel
Current Use	Luxury resort "Amadria Park Šibenik"
Distribution of property	owned by Amadria Park Hotels
Good to know	The complex was awarded the "Borba" Federal Award for Architecture in 1967.

Located just a few kilometres outside the city of Šibenik, the Solaris hotel complex was developed from 1967. It consisted of a system of independent hotel clusters embedded in landscaped pine forests. Between 1967 and 1969, architect Boris Magaš planned three hotel buildings blending into the coastal landscape as flat white cuboids. The initial design was highly praised by architecture critics. In the following years, further hotels were added to the complex without Magaš's approval.

Like all major hotels, the resort became a shelter for refugees from Bosnia and Herzegovina during the Yugoslav War. After the war, the complex was restored for tourism purposes.

Today, the resort is presented under the name "Amadria Park Šibenik" including countless leisure and sports facilities, a convention centre and an artificial "authentic Dalmation village". Some of the original architecture was redesigned beyond recognition.

photo Bernadette Krejs

09

Ex. Hotel Complex
Marina Lučica
Primošten

•8

Architect	Lovro Perković
Built	1969–1972
Renovated	–
Original Use	Hotel
Current Use	vacant
Distribution of property	Company "Primošten" d.d., since 2002 Hungarian majority owner, no investment since the purchase.
Good to know	The beach in front of the hotel used to be a nudist beach.

Opposite the old town of Primošten, with a direct access road from the Adriatic Highway, lies what is now the ruins of the former Marina Lučica hotel. Designed by Lovro Perković and opened in the summer of 1971, the 21.000 m² building with 260 hotel rooms fits into the topography of Primošten bay, making it barely visible from the road. The hotel entrance was on street level, where also the reception, bar, and restaurant were located. The terraced rooms were cascaded and built into the hillside like ribbons. All hotel rooms had a view of the sea and the old town of Primošten. Framing the view played a crucial role in the design of the entire project.

The hotel was closed during the Yugoslav War in 1991 and served as a refugee shelter. After that, it was never reopened and since 2002, its majority owner is a Hungarian corporation which has made no further investment since the purchase.

photo Bernadette Krejs

"On entering the lobby, guests immediately enjoyed a framed image of the seaside horizon, the silhouette of a Venetian village on a peninsula at a distance. In the best case, the sun would even set behind its campanile."

Michael Zinganel
From "Social Tourism" to a Mass Market Consumer Paradise, p. 50–53.

10

Ex. Motel Sljeme Trogir [Motel Soline]
Trogir

Architect	Ivan Vitić
Built	1964–1965
Renovated	–
Original Use	Motel
Current Use	vacant / informal use
Distribution of property	longstanding lawsuit due to ownership dispute
Good to know	listed as heritage since 2013

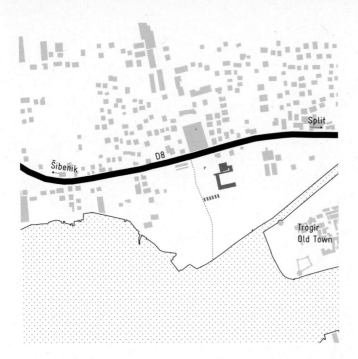

43°31'03.2"N
16°14'40.2"E
43.517556 | 16.244500
Ul. Kardinala
Alojzija Stepinca 23,
21220 Trogir

The Motel Soline in Trogir is one of three motels built by architect Ivan Vitić on behalf of the Yugoslav agricultural industrial combine Sljeme. All three motels, in Preluka near Rijeka, Biograd na Moru, and Trogir, were inaugurated in 1965, the same year the Adriatic Highway, along which they are located, was finished.

Vitić, an avid driver, designed his motels in terms of the needs and requirements of a motorist passing through. Instead of setting up a single large structure, he divided the functions into several compact elements: a main building with a reception and restaurant on the ground floor, and two annexes with further motel rooms. These elements can be accessed individually (by car) and are connected by covered paths. A characteristic feature of the motel in Trogir are six additional detached bungalows, each with their own parking space. Like the motel in Preluka near Rijeka, the stone wall is a major design element, but here a different formation was used (cyclopean masonry). The low building density on a very large area (20,000 m²) allowed for agricultural use of small fields on the site.
Previously owned by workers, the motel was sold during the privatisation process of the 1990s. Today, however, different owners lay claim to it. The motel has been left to decay with occasional informal use since.
In 2013, the NGO "Loose Associations" initiated the project "Motel Trogir", which aimed to obtain monument protection status for Vitić's motels, as well as to raise awareness of the architectural legacy of post-war modernity. The motels in Trogir (2013) and Rijeka (2015) were indeed listed as cultural heritage thanks to the initiative, but their future is still uncertain due to many aggravating circumstances. The motel in Biograd, the last one in operation, was unfortunately demolished in July 2019.

"Late Modernist architecture dating from the highly productive period between the 1950s and the 1980s, during which Croatia was part of the Socialist Federal Republic of Yugoslavia, has only become a subject of interest to the state monument protection administration in the last ten years."

Nataša Bodrožić & Lidija Butković Mićin
Motel Trogir: Saving the Past Futures, p. 78–81.

Site Map
Trogir

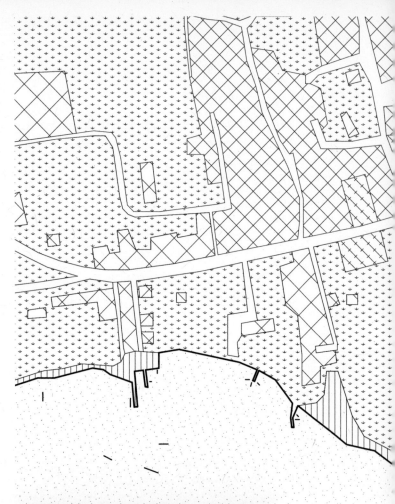

•9

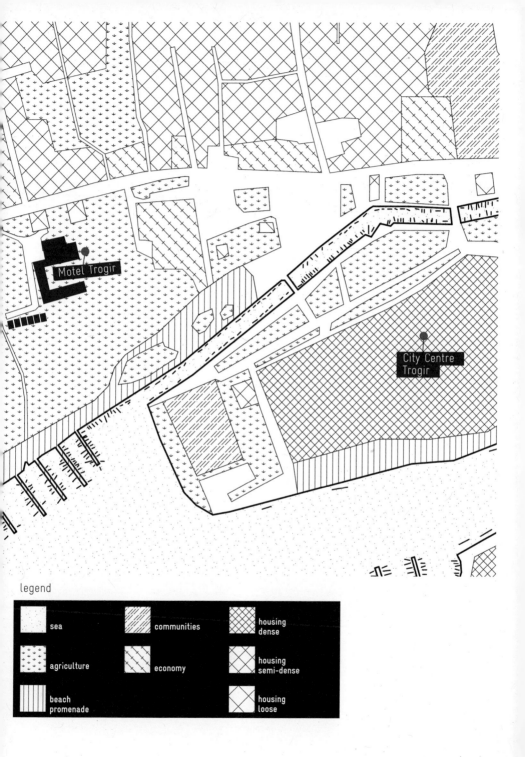

Motel Trogir

City Centre
Trogir

legend

sea	communities	housing dense
agriculture	economy	housing semi-dense
beach promenade		housing loose

Typology of Motel Sljeme Trogir
1964

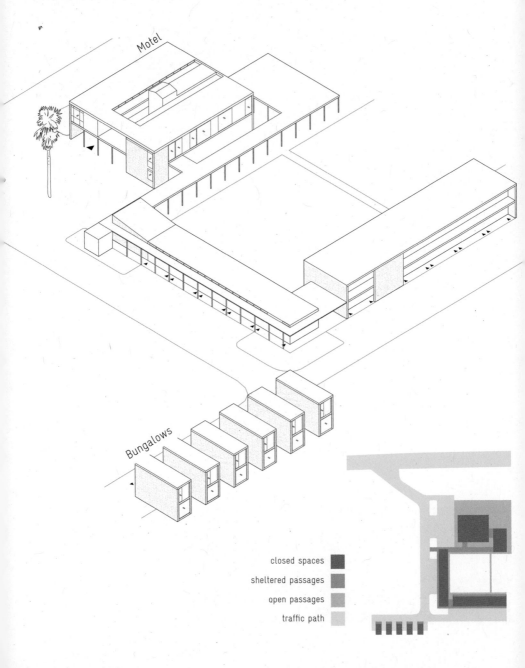

Motel

Bungalows

closed spaces
sheltered passages
open passages
traffic path

ground floor
1964

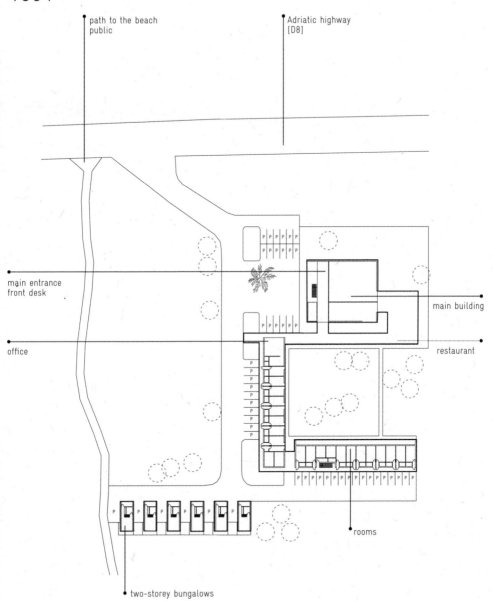

path to the beach
public

Adriatic highway
[D8]

main entrance
front desk

main building

office

restaurant

two-storey bungalows

rooms

Timeline
Motel Sljeme Trogir

direct relation ┊ indirect relation

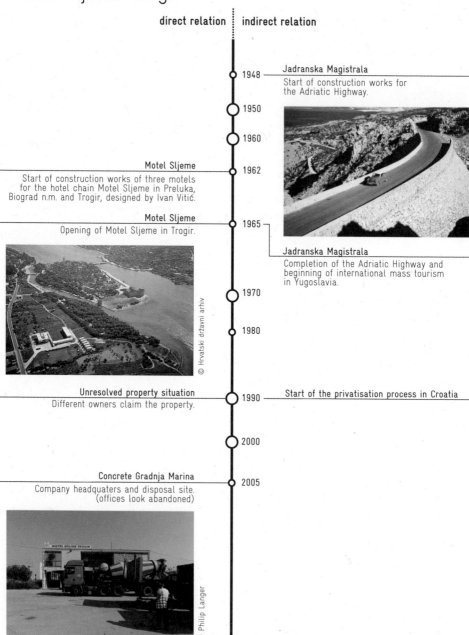

1948 — **Jadranska Magistrala**
Start of construction works for
the Adriatic Highway.

1950

1960

Motel Sljeme — **1962**
Start of construction works of three motels
for the hotel chain Motel Sljeme in Preluka,
Biograd n.m. and Trogir, designed by Ivan Vitić.

Motel Sljeme — **1965**
Opening of Motel Sljeme in Trogir.

Jadranska Magistrala
Completion of the Adriatic Highway and
beginning of international mass tourism
in Yugoslavia.

© Buro Griesbach

1970

1980

© Hrvatski državni arhiv

Unresolved property situation — **1990** — Start of the privatisation process in Croatia
Different owners claim the property.

2000

Concrete Gradnja Marina — **2005**
Company headquaters and disposal site.
(offices look abandoned)

© Philip Langer

76

Informal housing

Two homeless men and a dog live at the property.

© Joana Gritsch

Cultural Heritage of Croatia

In December 2013, the motel was listed as heritage.

Stolen Future

In December 2014, artist Neli Ružić designed a light art installation at Motel Soline. It was the first art intervention of many that emerged within the framework of the "Motel Trogir" project.

© Motel Trogir

Signage

After an open competition, the signage for Motel Soline and the Children's Health Resort Krvavica (designed by Jan Pavlović) were set up in space.

2006

2013

2014

2016

2018

Initiative "Motel Trogir" by NGO "Loose Associations"

The goal was placing the Motel Sljeme in Trogir under protection, as well as raising awareness for modernist architecture from the period of Socialist Yugoslavia.

"Motel Trogir: It is not future that always comes after"

In March 2014, the Initiative Motel Trogir published a book, a collection of texts revolving around Vitić's motel-chain and its socio-historic embedding.

Betonski Spavači

The documentary series "Betonski Spavači" (engl. Slumbering Concrete) was broadcast on state television. The second episode "Brief Encounters Along the Adriatic Highway" is about Motel Trogir.

© Irena Atanasova

Motel Trogir
Saving the Past Futures
Lidija Butković Mićin & Nataša Bodrožić

Nataša Bodrožić
is a curator and cultural
worker from Zagreb and
Trogir, Croatia. She is the
initiator and co-founder of
the Motel Trogir project, as
well as Loose Associations,
a contemporary art
platform. A strong believer
in collaborative creation,
she co-edited several books
in the field of contemporary
art, cultural policy and
heritage activism, such
as "Politics of Feelings /
Economies of Love" (2014),
"Motel Trogir:
It Is Not Future that
Always Comes After"
(2016), "Modelling Public
Space(s) in Culture:
Rethinking Institutional
Practices in Culture and
Historical (Dis) Continuities"
(2018) etc.

Lidija Butković Mićin
is an art historian
working as a research
assistant at the Department
of Art History, University
of Zadar, Croatia and is a
member of the Motel Trogir
project team. She publishes
articles on the history
of Croatian modernist
architecture, public
monuments, and visual arts.
She authored the exhibition
and the accompanying
book "Ada Felice-Rošić and
Nada Šilović: a Woman's
Touch in the Architectural
History of Rijeka" (City
Museum of Rijeka, 2014).

What is Motel Trogir?

The Motel Trogir project was launched in 2013 by Loose Associations – a platform for contemporary art practices, and its associates (Nataša Bodrožić, Lidija Butković Mićin and Saša Šimpraga, with the local support of Diana Magdić) – as a civil campaign focused on the motel built in Trogir in 1965, designed by Ivan Vitić, one of the most prominent Croatian architects of the 20th century. Vitić's motel is a rare example of outstanding modern architecture in Trogir, a mid-Dalmatian coastal town with approx. 13,000 permanent inhabitants, of whom approx. 1,000 live in its historical centre inscribed on the UNESCO World Heritage List since 1997. The project consists of many activities and has developed a specific methodology which can be described as a combination of civic activism and academic, publishing and educational work, including curating and producing contemporary art projects.

The Motel Trogir project | origins

Late Modernist architecture dating from the highly productive period between the 1950s and the 1980s, during which Croatia was part of the Socialist Federal Republic of Yugoslavia (SFRY), has only become a subject of interest to the state monument protection administration in the last ten years – an interest that is however expressed sporadically and primarily in the larger urban centres. For instance, the City Institute for the Protection of Cultural Monuments and Nature of the City of Zagreb has so far placed approximately thirty representative examples of post-World War II Modernism under its protection, thus taking the national lead in terms of the number of protected monuments, whereas in Split, where a more systematic registration of the structures dating from the interwar Modernist period has already been carried out, the registration and protection of more recent architectural achievements has only just begun. This part of the architectural legacy is still neglected – a heritage without an heir [1] – and all too often subjected to inadequate adaptation or accelerated decay due to insufficient (or non-existing) formal legal protection, undeveloped social awareness or questionable privatisation procedures which took place in the 1990s. The situation is especially difficult in smaller towns, particularly those with a rich architectural heritage where experts and conservators are focussed on monuments from earlier historical periods, leaving the overlooked Modernist architecture vulnerable. The Motel Trogir project of the Loose Associations has become part of the activities in the domestic non-institutional arena undertaken by civil society associations that have recognised the need for a stronger engagement in this field, primarily in order to compensate for the lack of institutional concern, but also to broach the subject of the social valuation of the still often stigmatised Socialist era's tangible heritage. This was done not only for the purpose of canonising specific structures or architectural complexes, but also in order to preserve the cultural memory and social affirmation of Modernism and its influence and current significance. The direct incentive for the cooperation of the participants of the Motel Trogir project was provided by the publicity campaign for entering the former Sljeme motel in Trogir, built in 1965, into the List of Protected Cultural Goods of the Republic of Croatia, which proved successful. The motel in Trogir was granted the status of a permanently protected cultural good of the Republic of Croatia in 2013. The same status was granted to a motel in Rijeka in 2015, a variant of the same original design by Ivan Vitić, which made it the first architectural monument built after World War II under formal protection in Rijeka and its surroundings. The first phase of the project (2013–2016) is summarised and described in the project's first publication called MOTEL TROGIR: it is not future that always comes after (ed. Bodrožić, Šimpraga / Loose Associations, Onomatopee, Zagreb / Eindhoven, 2016)

"Phase two" of the project

The fourth year of the Motel Trogir project activities was marked by a new initiative. In the beginning of 2016, we began the critical evaluation, interpretation and exploration of the possibilities for the protection of the famous Split point de repère, the Koteks Gripe sports and commercial centre (1979–1981), designed by Živorad Janković and Slaven Rožić. After Ivan Vitić's Adriatic coast motels in Trogir and Rijeka, the Koteks Gripe complex posed a completely different challenge. Therefore, the required method of action was also somewhat different. In February 2016, we sent a letter to the Department of Conservation in Split with the proposal of placing the complex under protection as one of the foremost architectural and urbanistic accomplishments of modern Split. At that point, we did not mention the degree of protection and we had already come up with a respectably long list of signatories, primarily architects, cultural workers and Split citizens, who willingly supported the initiative. The response of the Conservation Department in Split to this letter actually confirmed that for the City of Split's architecture and infrastructure, Koteks Gripe was extremely valuable, but we were told that it is a work of architects whose oeuvre is still to be scientifically processed and evaluated. This means that there was not enough knowledge gathered to provide a base for the reassessment of the mentioned complex. Therefore, just

[1]
The term was coined in the 1960s by Milan Prelog, Ph.D. (1919–1988.), a prolific Croatian art historian and an outspoken advocate for the preservation of historic architectural monuments endangered by large infrastructure projects and urban development in Croatia's coastal towns and villages due to accelerated economic growth. It has since become widely used in public debates aiming to point out any part of Croatia's national heritage that has suffered from the neglect of the proper authorities and/or the general public.

like in the case of Vitić's Adriatic motels, we decided to fill this gap and compile the first publication ever about this landmark.

Consumer Culture Ladscape in social Yugoslavia. The publication.
Starting from Koteks Gripe in Split, the research took us to three other ex-Yugoslav cities. Simultaneously we began to look into the political, social and economic context which enabled the appearance of four extraordinary buildings, all related to one of the co-authors of the Split complex. The publication, in a way, looks at Yugoslav consumerism through the lens of four ground-breaking buildings by Sarajevo architect Živorad Janković, a pioneer of socialist mixed use. Socialist Yugoslavia was a unique experiment with progressive social forms that were matched by a specific urban development. The mid-1960s to the country's disintegration in the 1990s is a period of ambiguity: while according to some researchers, the market-oriented economic reforms brought a much needed opening and liberalisation, to others it marked the beginning of the end of the revolutionary demand for equality. Thus, the anti-utopianism of the consumer welfare was reflected in the rise of the middle class with its recognisable habits and taste. Following a specific architectural typology, this book delves into this period that brought such social and economic change. It focuses on the sports and shopping centre Koteks Gripe in Split and similar architectural complexes in Sarajevo, Novi Sad, and Prishtina, all designed by Sarajevo-based architect Živorad Janković and associates, gradually expanding towards broader considerations of the architectural practice, contention and coalescence within the Yugoslav Modernist project.

Motel Trogir project: Echoes
Looking back at almost seven years of the project and continuous production of knowledge, art works, campaigns, relations, it is clear that the Motel Trogir project opened some new fields of interest, of action and engagement, but also became a point of reference for many other projects and (cultural) actors. It created some side effects as well, some that no one could have expected when we started the project. Let us mention only a few, to stress the project's flow, in lieu of a conclusion:

Following the committed approach of the Motel Trogir project in the local community (in Trogir), an independent activist group – Citizens Action Trogir (GAT) – was established, focusing on the spatial problems and public properties of the city of Trogir. Some of the joint actions it launched include the initiative for the reconstruction and maintenance of the historic park of Garagnin Fanfogna, the return of public fountains and the effort to preserve the green zone of "Soline" in the immediate vicinity of Vitić's motel.

An important part of our preservation strategy is the continuous production of cultural events and the promotion of the image of an endangered site through social media, publications and public posters for these events to oppose the prevailing "strategy of decay". In 2014, an international public call for proposals on the production of several site-specific artworks was launched. Ever since, the project is actively involved in producing and curating art works; with these activities pursued in parallel to the public campaigns and research. Meanwhile, several art works produced within (or in close relation with) the Motel Trogir project have become part of the collections of public museums in Croatia: a video installation entitled Stolen Future by artist Neli Ružić entered the Museum of Contemporary Art in Zagreb, and the Koteks Gripe photo work by Duška Boban the Museum of Fine Arts in Split.

From the very beginning, the Motel Trogir project has been communicating internationally, with a special focus on post-socialist and Mediterranean countries. Following the Motel Trogir activities abroad, especially its work on establishing the Mediterranean Modernism Network, and inciting collaborations in countries of northern Africa (Morocco, Algeria, Tunisia), a new organisation was founded in Morocco based on the model of the Motel Trogir project. After our meeting in Casablanca, architects from the Ecole d'Architecture de Casablanca founded an organisation named MAMMA_Mémoire des Architectes Modernes Marocains with similar goals for the preservation of the 20th century architectural heritage in Morocco.

»
photo Nataša Bodrožić

"Mapping shows us a way to understand spatial phenomena, it displays unseen and often immaterial areas, it reveals narratives (of a site) or indicates change and transformation."

Bernadette Krejs
Mapping as a Research Method in Architecture, p. 126–129.

← Split

Day 04 around Split

County Split-Dalmatia
Population 178,102 [City] | 240,298 [Urban]
346,314 [Metro][2011]
Area 79.33 km²

Split is the largest city in Dalmatia. The
origins of the city can be traced back to
Diocletian's Palace built in the 4th century
AD. In the city structure, all the historical
layers from ancient Rome through the
Middle Ages to the present day are visible
and alive. The palace and the city centre
were declared a UNESCO World Heritage
Site in 1979. But Split is much more than
a magnificent architectural scenery.
Although age is so prevalent, it is a
surprisingly young city. In the old town,
there are many hip bars and you can find
many cultural events such as film and
theatre festivals, exhibitions or museums.

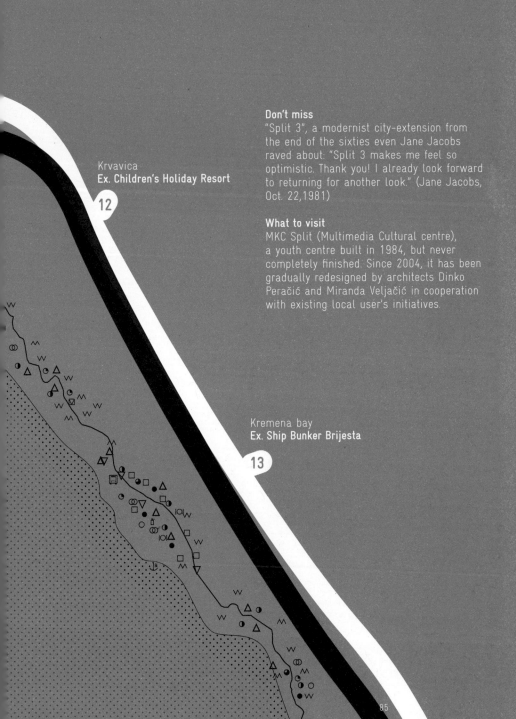

Krvavica
Ex. Children's Holiday Resort

12

Kremena bay
Ex. Ship Bunker Brijesta

13

Don't miss
"Split 3", a modernist city-extension from
the end of the sixties even Jane Jacobs
raved about: "Split 3 makes me feel so
optimistic. Thank you! I already look forward
to returning for another look." (Jane Jacobs,
Oct. 22,1981)

What to visit
MKC Split (Multimedia Cultural centre),
a youth centre built in 1984, but never
completely finished. Since 2004, it has been
gradually redesigned by architects Dinko
Peračić and Miranda Veljačić in cooperation
with existing local user's initiatives.

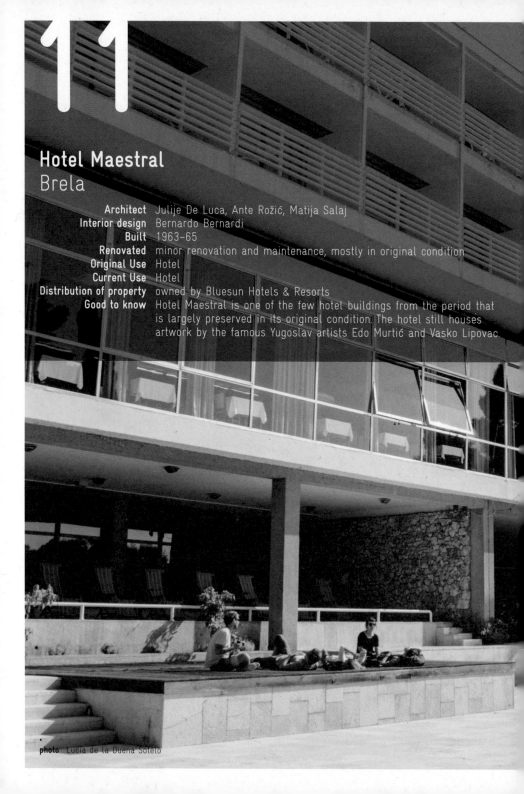

11

Hotel Maestral
Brela

Architect	Julije De Luca, Ante Rožić, Matija Salaj
Interior design	Bernardo Bernardi
Built	1963–65
Renovated	minor renovation and maintenance, mostly in original condition
Original Use	Hotel
Current Use	Hotel
Distribution of property	owned by Bluesun Hotels & Resorts
Good to know	Hotel Maestral is one of the few hotel buildings from the period that is largely preserved in its original condition. The hotel still houses artwork by the famous Yugoslav artists Edo Murtić and Vasko Lipovac.

photo Lucia de la Dueña Sotelo

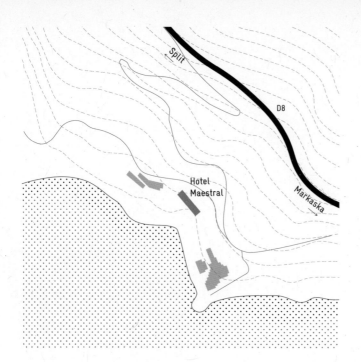

43°22'09.4"N
16°55'43.8"E
43.369278 | 16.928833

Filipinska 1,
21322 Brela

The Hotel Maestral in Brela was part of a local urban development plan in 1962, which was developed by the same team of architects who planned the hotel (De Luca, Rožić and Salaj). It follows a strategy of compact and small volumes which are carefully embedded in the topography, the vegetation and the environment.

According to the idea of a holistic architecture, the interior design and decor of Hotel Maestral was designed in cooperation with architect and designer Bernardo Bernardi. The volume of the building, a horizontal block, lies between two slight elevations in a slope. The main orientation, both the rooms and and the terraces, is towards the sea. The upper part of the building, in which the rooms are located, projects slightly beyond the lower area of the lobby, the bar and restaurant, allowing it to stand out clearly.

The precise handling of materials and shapes makes it a special masterpiece of the post-war tourist architecture of Yugoslavia. The hotel is still in use and is mostly preserved in its original condition.

12

Ex. Children's Holiday Resort Kravica
Baška Voda, Krvavica

Architect	Rikard Marasović, Slobodan Kasiković
Built	1963–1964
Renovated	–
Original Use	Holiday resort for children with lung diseases, built and managed by the Yugoslav People's Army; from the 1970s until the 1990s, it operated as "normal" military holiday resort.
Current Use	vacant, a small part is still inhabited
Distribution of property	Republic of Croatia, currently managed by Ministry of State Property
Good to know	listed as heritage since 2015

photo: Michael Lindinger

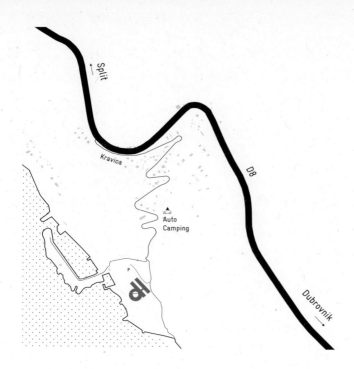

The Children's Resort in in Krvavica was built on behalf of the Yugoslav People's Army (JNA) for children with lung diseases. Situated in the midst of pine forests between sea and mountains, it seems as if an extraterrestrial Something had landed: a circular volume levitates and nestles between the treetops.

The design originally was by architect Rikard Marasović who left the project due to disagreements with the principal. The architectural office "Centroprojekt Beograd" took over, with Slobodan Kasiković as project leader. After the construction had begun in 1963, an earthquake in Skopje led to stricter regulations in the region. A more stable construction was required and the statics had to be revised. This resulted in a delay of the construction work, so the building wasn't completed until its inauguration in 1965.

The complex consists of three buildings – a circular main building, a storage area, and a residential wing for the staff. In the circular upper floor of the main building, which seems to float on its columns, are the children's bedrooms. There, double-sided natural lighting and ventilation were created by a fold in the ceiling. The building was designed to function as a natural healing apparatus using wind, sun and nature. In 1974, the JNA decided to abandon the original function as a children's hospital and turned it into a hotel for its employees. In the 1980s, it was even expanded with prefabricated bungalows in the surrounding pine forest. During the Yugoslav War, it was used as a refugee shelter. Since then, the main building has been vacant, but the eight apartments of the former staff section are still inhabited. The ownership of the complex is still unclear, and its future, as with so many others, is uncertain. The efforts of the local municipal administration to demolish the building and establish a luxury tourism resort failed as the building was listed as heritage in 2015.

photo Manfred Wuits

Timeline
Children's Holiday Resort Krvavica

May 1965
Opening of the military holiday facility for children with lung diseases.

1974
In 1974, the facility was repurposed into a military hotel.

1991
The Croatian army takes over the facility.

1990s
Repurposing as refugee camp.

2000s
The main building is abandoned, vandalism and informal appropriation follow.

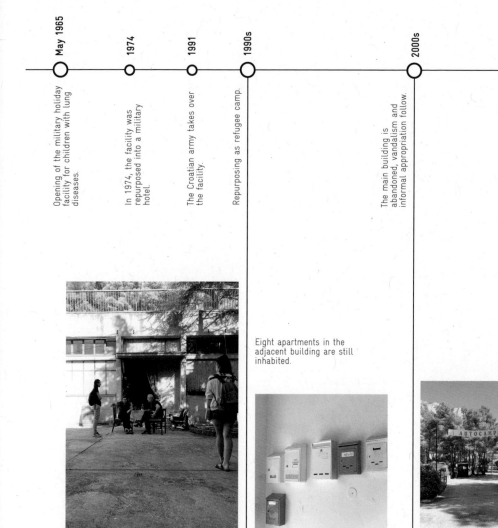

Eight apartments in the adjacent building are still inhabited.

2015

2018

The building is listed as
cultural heritage.

Tenants attempt to buy their
apartments. Ownership:
Republic of Croatia

Fast food restaurants,
marina and a
camping site next to
the ruin.

Public beach and marina are
used by the locals.

Typology
Children's Holiday Resort

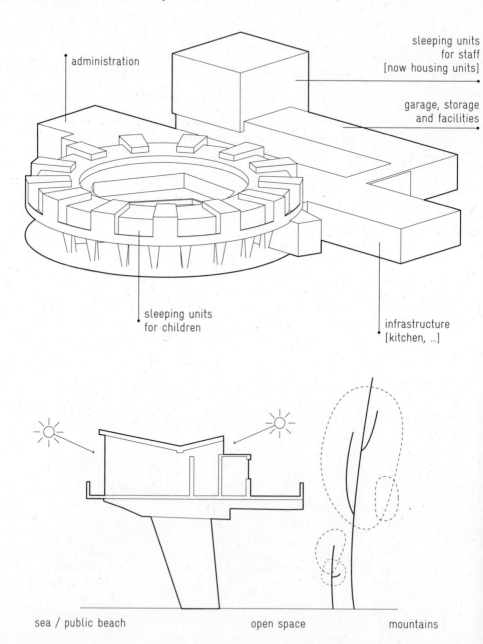

administration

sleeping units
for staff
[now housing units]

garage, storage
and facilities

sleeping units
for children

infrastructure
[kitchen, ...]

sea / public beach   open space   mountains

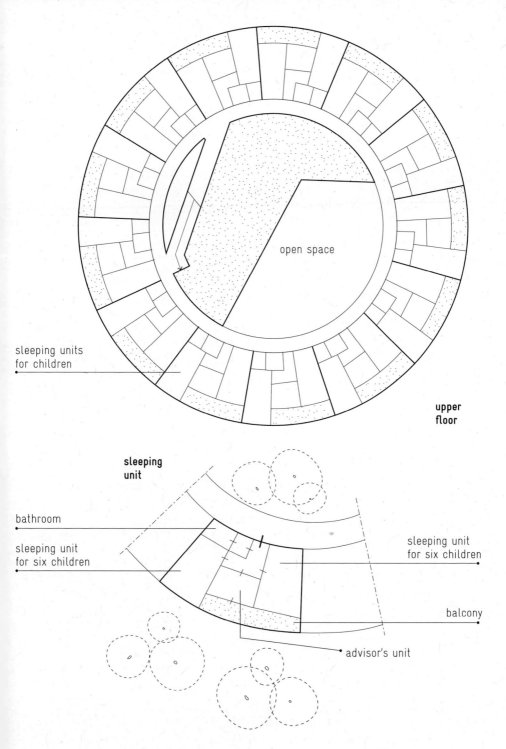

open space

sleeping units
for children

upper floor

sleeping unit

bathroom

sleeping unit
for six children

sleeping unit
for six children

balcony

advisor's unit

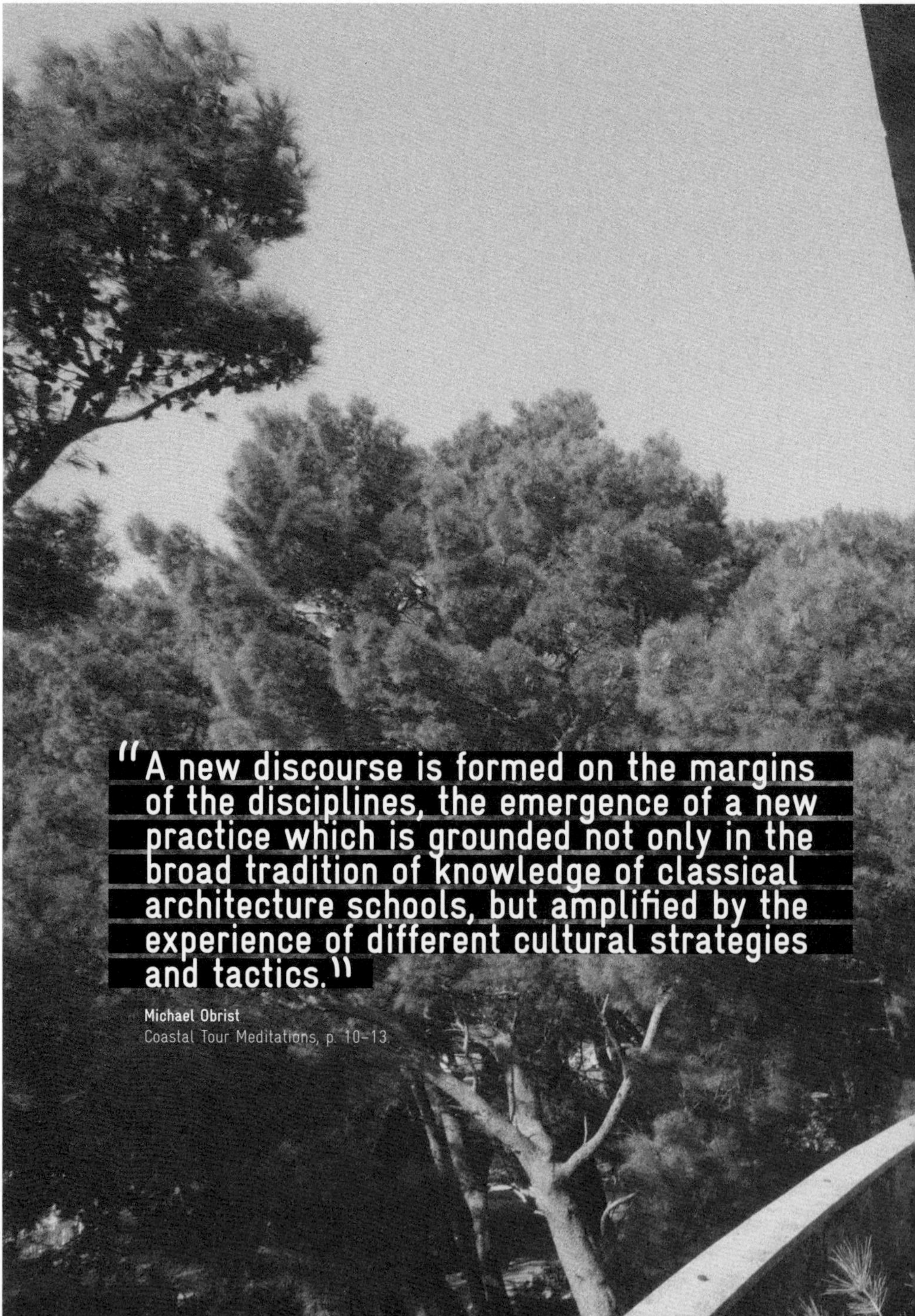

"A new discourse is formed on the margins of the disciplines, the emergence of a new practice which is grounded not only in the broad tradition of knowledge of classical architecture schools, but amplified by the experience of different cultural strategies and tactics."

Michael Obrist
Coastal Tour Meditations, p. 10–13

photo Maria Groiss

13

Ex. Ship Bunker Brijesta
Kremena bay,
municipality of Slivno,
south of Ploče

•10

Architect	unknown
Built	approximately between 1950 and 1970
Renovated	-
Original Use	bunker for warships
Current Use	informal use as mooring place, swimming
Distribution of property	Republic of Croatia; managed by the Croatian Ministry of Defence
Good to know	There is a very similar ship bunker "Duba" in the neighbouring bay.

Brijesta near Ploče is one of several ship bunkers located along the Croatian coast, built by the Yugoslav People's Army during the Cold War. Usually the bunkers were blasted into the rock and partially concreted. All ship bunkers were implemented according to standardised plans, which were adapted to the respective local conditions. So they differ slightly in size, depth and in the design of their openings. In the case of the Brijesta ship bunker, metal wings, which could be pivoted for camouflage purposes, were attached to the entrance.
When exactly the ship bunker was built is not clear from the literature, due to long-term military secrecy. The bunker buildings are under the administration of the Croatian Ministry of Defense today, but out of use. Brijesta is occasionally used by local fishermen as a boat mooring. Right in the neighbouring bay, there is a similar ship bunker named "Duba".

photo Maria Groiss

Mobility
along the Croatian coast
in different types of locomotion

Illustration by
Joana Gritsch,
Cristina Krois

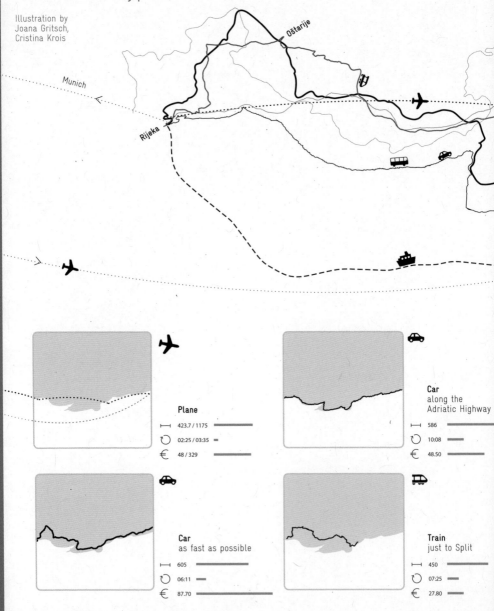

Munich

Oštarije

Rijeka

Plane
⊢ 423.7 / 1175
⟳ 02:25 / 03:35
€ 48 / 329

Car
along the
Adriatic Highway
⊢ 586
⟳ 10:08
€ 48.50

Car
as fast as possible
⊢ 605
⟳ 06:11
€ 87.70

Train
just to Split
⊢ 450
⟳ 07:25
€ 27.80

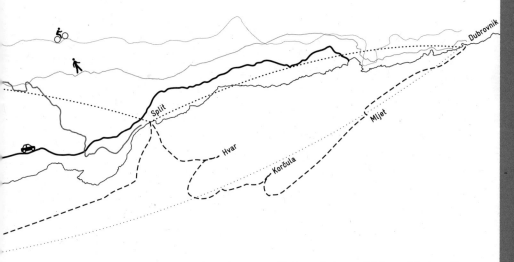

Distance between Rijeka and Dubrovnik
linear distance   418.93 km

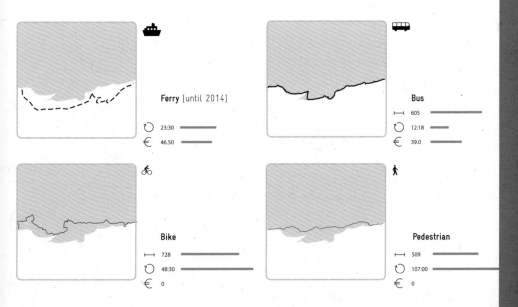

Ferry [until 2014]

↻ 23:30 ▬▬▬
€ 46.50 ▬▬▬

Bus

⊢⊣ 605 ▬▬▬
↻ 12:18 ▬▬
€ 39.0 ▬▬

Bike

⊢⊣ 728 ▬▬▬▬
↻ 48:30 ▬▬▬▬
€ 0

Pedestrian

⊢⊣ 509 ▬▬▬
↻ 107:00 ▬▬▬▬▬
€ 0

Constructing a Travel Landscape
Opposing Ambitions Shaping the Ground
of the Eastern Adriatic Coast
Melita Čavović

Melita Čavlović,
postdoctoral associate
at the Department of
Theory and History of
Architecture at the
Faculty of Architecture,
University of Zagreb. She
was an active researcher
on the scientific project
"Atlas of the 20th Century
Croatian Architecture".
Her scholarly work is
devoted to the research
of the circumstances
informing and guiding the
architectural and urban
postwar production.

Once finally traced on the ground, the winding route of the more than 800 km-long Adriatic Highway has permanently transformed the territory of the Eastern Adriatic coast. Connecting the scattered sequence of coastal towns and settlements for the first time since antiquity, it initiated a series of irreversible processes we witness even today. This brief account will merely accentuate some of the crucial developments of the numerous conflicting visions that arose both from the ground and the planning tables, exasperated even further by numerous economic, political, legal and societal ambitions that are yet to be resolved.

The narrow coastal strip of the Eastern Adriatic has a complex heritage marked by profound historical and political discontinuity. It was comprised, primarily, of a multitude of towns and villages separated by large swaths of uninhabited or even inhospitable Mediterranean landscape marked by natural characteristics distinctly different from one region to another. Furthermore, this sliver of coastal terrain is physically cut off from the hinterland by a series of mountain ranges stretching from north to south, with only a handful of geographically viable connections to the Pannonian basin. These strategic linkages were traditionally more important and far easier to construct than the continuous route along the coast. This journey, and with it the experience of travelling along the Adriatic as a totality, was made possible only after World War II, and the completion of the highway. Previously, this was possible only to a privileged few who were so fortunate as to perceive this territory from the deck of an elite tourist steamship.

Adding to the complexity and inhospitality of the topography are the political obstacles to any sustained attempt of connecting this territory. From a historical perspective, this territory was never under a single political governance, with a multitude of empires, dominions and independent municipalities vying for supremacy. It was only after the end of World War II that the conditions for its actual unification were met. Prior to it, there was no common national interest that would build the necessary transport network since the people inhabiting the coast lived separately, traditionally inheriting opposing cultures, they were subjected to divergent and often opposing strategies of development stemming from the varying priorities of colonial centres that governed them.

Initially only a civil engineering endeavor, the construction of the Adriatic Highway, which in effect was a humble two-lane road with an average width of about 7 m, was anything but an easy accomplishment. Insufficient federal funding was the reason why road reconstruction was which prevented over the construction of new roads, prohibiting the finalisation of new segments of the route. The first capital investment directed towards the construction of the highway was distributed as late as 1959, at which point a mere 50% of the road had been completed. The initial cost estimate for its completion was made for a route stretching from Koper all the way to Bar, connecting five Yugoslav Republics, with the largest portion passing through the Socialist Republic of Croatia. This provisional calculation — which relied heavily on segments of pre-existing roads — soon became inadequate and in 1961, a new one was presented since the course of the highway as executed on the ground began to deviate rapidly from the plans and tended to follow the coastal line more closely. These departures were intentional and at times were chosen to circumvent fertile agricultural land or to avoid passing through existing towns where the built fabric prevented any future broadening of its roadbed. Initially only a welcome outcome, but soon a crucial route-tracing strategy was the discovery of previously unimaginable tourist attractions in the vast stretches of pristine nature that was now easily accessible and attracted a growing number of tourists with each finished segment. The sudden increase in arrivals that followed the highway as it was being finished went hand in hand with praise of the scenic qualities of the winding route that was unfolding in front of the visitors. The discovery of the joy of traveling along the highway was compared to watching a movie framed by the windshield of a car. This ever-changing sequence that now presented itself to motorised visitors offered previously hidden vistas. For the first time now, masses of people were able to see the multitude of coastal towns that before had only been accessible by sea from the other side, from the mainland, and from the safety of a car.

Since the beauty of the coast, as revealed by the newly constructed highway, began to attract a rising number of tourists, this emerging economy began to come in conflict with the nation-wide industrialisation project which was central to all spatial development strategies. It was almost religiously believed — both on the basis of prevailing planning theories and as observed from initial successful attempts around the country — that industrial development was the only sustainable way to bring about economic prosperity for poor regions. As opposed to industry, tourism revenues varied throughout the year in relation to the seasons, so it could not guarantee the continuous employment of local workers and was not perceived as economically viable. The massive and almost immediate touristification of the eastern Adriatic coast, on the other hand, left Yugoslav officials entirely unprepared. Large industrial complexes, either as already built

Celmić, Ivan. "Jadranska magistrala." Ceste i mostovi 51, no. 1–3 (2005): 89–98.

Čavlović, Melita, Antun Sevšek and Damir Gamulin. "Sequencing the Adriatic Highway in Croatia from 1965 to 1990: Textual Mapping of a Linear Territory." Presentation at the conference From Building to Continent: How Architecture makes Territories, Canterbury, UK, 2018.

Čavlović, Melita. "The motel and the Adriatic highway." In Motel Trogir: it is not future that always comes after, edited by Nataša Bodrožić and Saša Šimpraga, 68-83. Zagreb and Eindhoven: Loose associations – Onomatopee, 2016.

Čavlović, Melita. "Constructing a travel landscape: A case study of the Sljeme motels along the Adriatic highway." Architectural Histories, no. 6, (2018): 1–14, doi.org/10.5334/ah.187.

International Bank for Reconstruction and Development. Appraisal of a Highway Project Yugoslavia. Washington: IBRD, International Development Association,1963.

Kečkemet, Duško. Jadranska magistrala. Rijeka Split Dubrovnik. Zagreb: Zajednica poduzeća za ceste SRH, 1965.

Šuvar, Stipe and Miroslav Jilek. "Sociološki aspekti turističkog razvoja na Jadranu." Arhitektura, no. 26 (1972): 4–6.

on the outskirts of large urban centres or as they were being planned, were in direct conflict with the nascent touristification – both from the perspective of competing for priority of use of valuable coastal land, and for their incompatibility with the highly desired spectacle of pastoral nature as advertised to the rising flood of motorists drawn southward to Dubrovnik as the most desired destination.

Yet another scale of spatial conflict arose from the fact that the actual completion of the highway, along with the explosive and haphazard construction of private tourist accommodation, preceded any systematic attempt of spatial planning control of development along the coast. Almost instantaneously with the finalisation of individual segments of the route, massive economic and demographic transformations were triggered that were soon reflected in the formation of a new kind of territory. This region promptly became characterised by both the lowest percentage of agricultural workers and the highest rate of internal migration in the entire country. This flux of people was predominantly directed from the hinterland towards the coast and most drastically pronounced in the Makarska region on the southern section of the route. Historical urban cores and traditional settlements that were previously surrounded by agricultural land and divided by inhospitable terrain were being joined in a continuous linear peri-urban landscape that started to be constructed along the coast. This explosive growth started around 1960 and was already well advanced by the opening of the last segment of the highway, celebrated in May 1965. The steep rise in tourism profits continued to baffle economic analysts as they witnessed the number of tourists during the summer soon eclipse the local population, with the Adriatic coast contributing a resounding 90 percent of all foreign currency tourist revenue in the country. The extent of these transformations was not only visible in the proliferation of new tourist typologies and their sheer numbers but also in a comprehensive modernisation process brought about by the influx of tourists enabled by the highway. The overwhelmingly poor inhabitants of the coastal region who had previously subsisted primarily on agriculture and fishing were now able to receive short-term loans they used to furnish their homes with modern appliances and enlarge them in order to accommodate tourists, dramatically transforming their lifestyles and living habits.

The sudden accessibility and desirability of the coast sparked a massive increase in domestic tourist arrivals, but the sheer volume of foreign currency that was instrumental in guiding the development of the country soon revealed a pronounced disparity between the tourist experience available to Yugoslavs as opposed to the visitors from the West. While considerable effort was being put into building state-of-the-art hotel complexes geared toward the more affluent foreign visitors, the bulk of domestic tourism was directed towards camps and bungalows with communal facilities constructed by the businesses and organisations people were employed by.

Almost a historical side note, and lost among the heroic proclamations of industrial and touristic development strategies in the local press, are the initial strategic considerations of the US intelligence agencies that were decisive for securing the approval of the UNDP loan that made the completion of the highway possible in the first place. Echoing these reports, almost the entire amount of funds dedicated to the reconstruction of road infrastructure in Yugoslavia in 1963, including the crucial Brotherhood and Unity Highway, were diverted to the Adriatic route. This funding was stipulated on the condition of creating a thoroughfare meeting the minimal military requirements for the rapid deployment of troops from Western Europe via Trieste, deep into the Balkan peninsula. But, as was the case with other demands put before the highway, the impassable terrain it had to cover soon forced the builders to abandon these considerations of military efficiency, settling for the humble 7-m roadbed along the entirety of the route.

All the processes listed above could be used as clues for understanding the processes evolving around the history of the Adriatic Highway in addition to being decisive vantage points for analysing the current situation. Since the road became the key driving force of an extensive modernisation of the coast, it also stimulated various divergent ambitions vying for the control of the future of these developments. Brought together under the common denominator of a new kind of continuously constructed landscape, these conflicts are tangible to the present day.

⌃ **Before and after the passage of the Highway.**
Collage by Melita Čavlović.
[https://ispu.mgipu.hr/, screenshot digital orthophoto map, 1968; screenshot Google Earth, December 3, 2014]

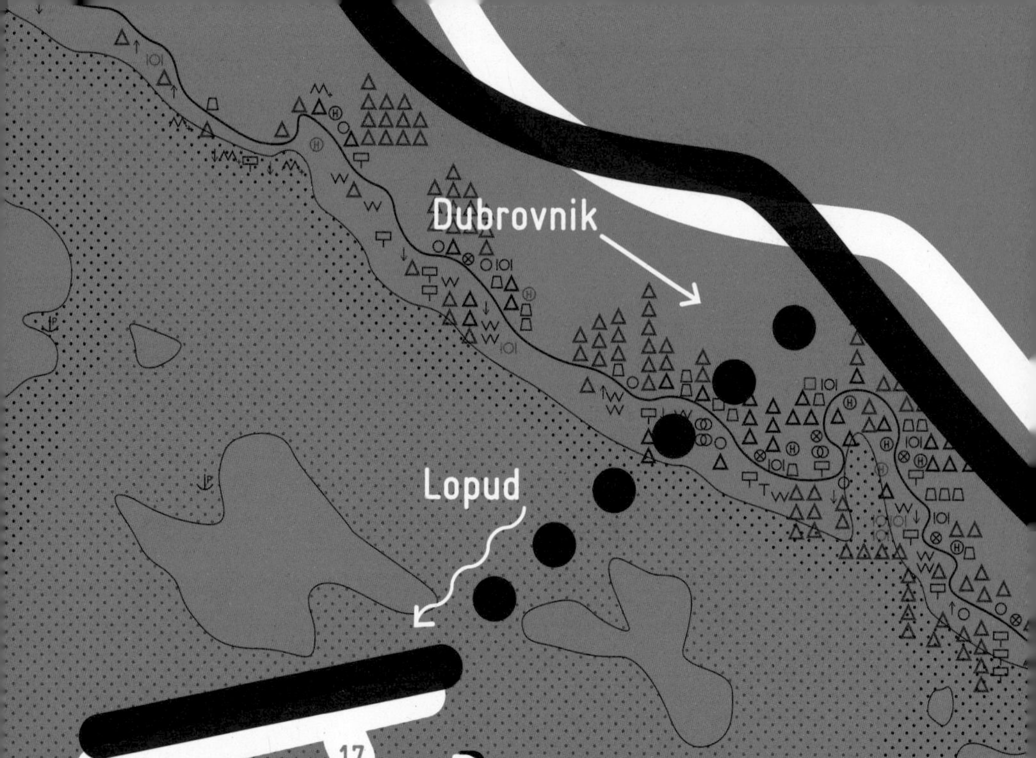

Dubrovnik

Lopud

Lopud
Ex. Grand Hotel

17

Day
05 around Dubrovnik

County Dubrovnik-Neretva
Population 42,615 [2011]
Area 143.35 km²

The Pearl of the Adriatic. With a nickname
like that, it is hard not to expect sheer
magnificence when visiting the old town of
Dubrovnik. With its imposing city walls, it
juts into the Adriatic Sea as a small fortress
and has been a UNESCO heritage since
1979. However, for a while now, Dubrovnik
has been overwhelmed by more and more
tourists. Every day, several cruise ships land
and spill their masses into the city. And
since Dubrovnik served as a backdrop to
the cult series Game of Thrones, even more
tourists are pouring into the city. Meanwhile,
specially designed tours are offered and fan
merchandise is sold.
At the beginning of the 1990s, the population
living in the old city centre counted 5,000
people, but today only 700 remain.

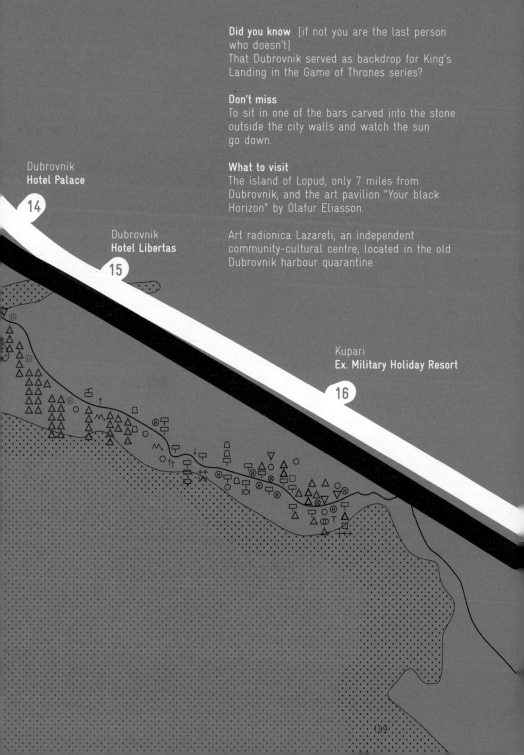

Did you know [if not you are the last person who doesn't]
That Dubrovnik served as backdrop for King's Landing in the Game of Thrones series?

Don't miss
To sit in one of the bars carved into the stone outside the city walls and watch the sun go down.

What to visit
The island of Lopud, only 7 miles from Dubrovnik, and the art pavilion "Your black Horizon" by Olafur Eliasson.

Art radionica Lazareti, an independent community-cultural centre, located in the old Dubrovnik harbour quarantine.

Dubrovnik
Hotel Palace

14

Dubrovnik
Hotel Libertas

15

Kupari
Ex. Military Holiday Resort

16

14

42°39'02.7"N
18°03'39.2"E
42.650750 | 18.060889
Masarykov put 20,
20000 Dubrovnik

Hotel Palace
Dubrovnik, Lapad

•11

Architect	Andrija Čičin-Šain, Žarko Vincek
Built	1969–1972
Renovated	2004 and 2014
Original Use	Hotel
Current Use	Hotel
Distribution of property	Adriatic Luxury Hotels

In 1968, a team consisting of Andrija Čičin-Šain and Žarko Vincek won two competitions for hotel architecture in the City of Dubrovnik. The first hotel to be finished, Hotel Palace, was inaugurated in 1972 on the hillside of Lapad. The entire building consists of a cascading concrete construction that follows the everted coastline by a slight direction-break of the volumes. The architects' concept provided modular housing units with terraces, that could be multiplied and assembled as required. A special feature of the hotel is its variety of courtyards. Due to disagreements with the hotel management, it became impossible to complete the interior design according to the wishes of the architects.
Hotel Palace was operated as a B category hotel until the 1990s. It was damaged during the Yugoslav Wars and stood empty for a while. After an initial renovation and reopening in 2004, the hotel was thoroughly renovated in 2014 by the Zagreb-based architecture office 3LHD.

photo Aline Eriksson

15

Hotel Libertas
Dubrovnik

•12

Architect	Andrija Čičin-Šain, Žarko Vincek
Interior Design	Raul Goldoni
Built	1968–1974
Renovated	2004–2007, incl. annexes
Original Use	Hotel
Current Use	Hotel
Distribution of property	Libertas Rixos Group

The design of Hotel Libertas resulted from a competition, as did the neighbouring Hotel Palace. The same team of architects convinced the jury. Following the topography of the coast, the concrete structure cascaded along the cliffs of the bay from top to bottom: the upper floors in a convex curve, the lower ones in a concave curve. Intensified by its green terraces, the building seemed to merge with the landscape. In the sense of a total design, the interior of the hotel was developed in collaboration with the sculptor Raul Goldoni, who also designed the structured partitions between the terraces (which unfortunately no longer exist).

In the wake of the Yugoslav Wars, the hotel was damaged and remained empty for many years as a kind of war memorial. In 2007, it underwent a major alteration and was reopened by the Turkish Rixos Group as "Rixos Libertas Dubrovnik".

Renovations in 2007 changed the hotel a lot. The basic structure was retained, but a floor was added above the entrance area, as well as a new annex with apartments. The beach zone, too, was expanded and the shape and proportions of terrace partitions changed.

photo Carina Bliem

16

Ex. Military Holiday Resort
Kupari

Architect The 6 hotels were planned by different architects, among them David Finc
[Hotel Pelegrin, Hotel Goričina I]

Built Grand Hotel [1920], Hotel Goričina [1962], Hotel Pelegrin [1963],
Hotel Kupari, Hotel Galeb, Hotel Mladost and Hotel Goričina II during the
1970s and 1980s

Renovated Several renovations and extensions until the 1980s / vacant since 1990s

Original Use holiday resort

Current Use vacant

Distribution of property Republic of Croatia, managed by Ministry of State Property,
current legal right of use: Avenue Group

Good to know The only hotel in Kupari listed as heritage is the Grand Hotel.

photo Carina Bliem

The first major hotel in Kupari was built by Czeck investors in 1920: the Grand Hotel. Since the 1960s it was complemented by 6 further hotels, built by the Yugoslav People's Army and intended to serve as a summer vacation resort for military employees and their families. After a few years, these hotels, and especially Hotel Pelegrin with its futuristic architectural language, became popular among international tourists as well. 2,000 beds and space for 4,000 campers were available in the heyday of the bay. The complex offered numerous entertainment and leisure facilities: a disco-club, a cinema, several restaurants, diverse indoor and outdoor sports courts. In Hotel Kupari, the largest facility according to the number of beds, there was also a swimming pool suitable for professional athletes. Kupari Resort served as a training camp for many professional sports clubs. Further in the west, there was a detached group of facilities: Hotel Galeb and two residential villas, Borovka I and II, with an underground shelter structure. This part of the facility is located within a restricted zone, today still used by the Croatian military.

During the siege of Dubrovnik in 1991, the complex was bombed. It hasn't been in operation since then, becoming more and more devastated over the following years.
There were several attempts by changing Croatian governments to revive this precious national property. The latest one, a competition launched in 2015, saw the Russian Avenue Group, headquartered in Vienna, as the only operator to gain legal rights to use the complex for 99 years. This also includes a concession of approximately 75,000 m² of the coastal zone. According to the latest announcements, the first guests should find accommodation in a new luxury resort by 2020. According to plans, only Grand Hotel, which dates back to 1920 will be renovated. The other hotels will be demolished and two new hotels and bungalow complexes will be built in their place. So far, however, nothing indicates this project is being realised, and the media is speculating about the termination of the contract.

photo Carina Bliem

Kupari Site

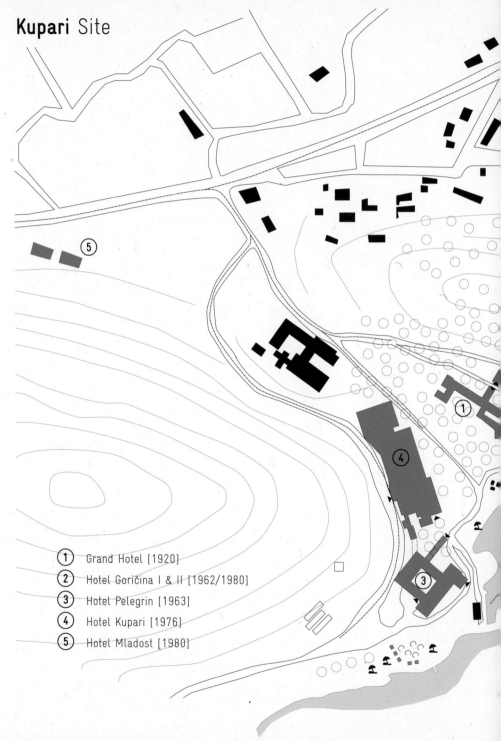

1. Grand Hotel [1920]
2. Hotel Goričina I & II [1962/1980]
3. Hotel Pelegrin [1963]
4. Hotel Kupari [1976]
5. Hotel Mladost [1980]

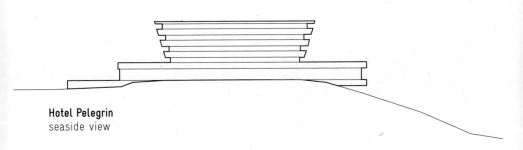

Hotel Pelegrin
seaside view

•13

photo
Carina Bilem

"Croatia's coastal belt is protected by law and must be freely accessible to all at all times. A privatisation of 'maritime property'* is prohibited, but concessions of up to 99 years can be sought."

Antonia Dika
Adriatic Coast Between Mass Tourism and Cold War, p. 38–41.
*[by law the area that can be reached by the highest wave during thunderstorms]

17

Ex. Grand Hotel
Lopud Island

•14

Architect	Nikola Dobrović
Built	1931–1936
Renovated	annex 1973
Original Use	Hotel
Current Use	vacant, temporary accommodation for workers
Distribution of property	Anker Grupa
Good to know	For the purpose of the construction of the Grand Hotel a quarry was established and a small concrete factory was built on the island.

The Grand Hotel on the island of Lopud is a beautiful example of pre-war modern tourist architecture. Architect Nikola Dobrović designed the hotel in the early 1930s for a family from the island. He describes the Grand Hotel as a functional machine. The floor plan is L-shaped and based on a concrete structure. The hotel is set back from the beach, leaving room for a garden. Building, construction, interior design, built-in room furnishings, and landscape design are all part of the architect's concept. The rooms are very small, and there are shared bathrooms on each floor.

After the World War II, private property was nationalised and the hotel was run by a state-owned hotel company. In a second construction phase in 1973, the existing building was renovated and an extension with larger rooms and private bathrooms was built.

From the 1980s, the hotel's condition deteriorated since the older rooms no longer met hotel standards, and guests stayed away. During the Yugoslav War, the hotel was occupied by combatants. After the war, the hotel was never reopened. The ownership situation changed several times and a partial renovation of the building was begun but never completed. In 2011, the hotel was sold to Anker Grupa, which also owns another hotel on the island.

photo Lucia de la Duena Sotelo

Mapping as a Research Method in Architecture
Bernadette Krejs

Bernadette Krejs
is a member of the
Research Unit of Housing
and Design / Institute of
Architecture and Design
at the Technical University
of Vienna. Her research
focuses on "Architecture as
Image – image production,
regimes and representation
in current architecture
production."
She lectured at the
Technical University
of Graz and was part of
the research project
"Intensified
Density – a small scale
densification strategy
for the suburbs by using
modular construction".
She is co-editor and author
of the book "Cartography
of Smallness – Learning
from Japan, Small-Scale
Densification Strategies for
Vienna." She aslo was
co-organizer of
the conference
CLAIMING*SPACES –
Feminist Perspectives in
Architecture and Spatial
Planning, at TU Vienna,
2019. She works and lives
in Vienna as an architect
and researcher.

Architecture often struggles with the idea of research. Why is that? If we look at its tools and methods, research in general all too often remains in the domain of the written word. Especially in architectural research, graphic work is a very suitable tool of knowledge production. Architectural research that uses visual tools – like drawings, plans, sketches, collages, diagrams and maps – seems obvious, because architects, designers and urbanists are much more familiar with these methods of representation.

The architectural drawing can be understood as a research tool, a valid form of investigating knowledge and meaning. The drawing can help us to understand, to intervene, to find out or to suggest spatial issues. "Drawing is not only an appropriate form of investigation, but one that allows for entirely different forms of knowledge to emerge." [1] So is there "graphic-based" research in architecture?

The very foundation of research is to ask questions, not simply to record things. In architectural research, we deal with spatial questions, for instance: how do we use space, how do we live, how do we inhabit space, who has access, and finally how do we design these spaces? These questions have an enormous impact on society, politics, and economy. In the research process, we are dealing with a broad complexity of available information and data. Finding appropriate and diverse forms of visualisation for an effective and democratic communication is an important challenge. Diagrams and maps are tools to understand certain phenomena and to make them legible for a broader audience through visualization. But data collections are often separated from lived experience and isolated from the geographical terrain. For architects, this constitutes rather a daunting problem because site, terrain, ground and landscape are among the most important components in the design process.

Architects and designers deal with a set of techniques like drawing, diagramming, cartography, etc. - which always involve the challenge of translating three-dimensional information onto a two-dimensional surface. The term "drawing" is an every-day term in a very broad category. Drawings offer the opportunity to translate things into another format. There are various visual appearances of drawings, some are very precise in dimension and measurement, others show the atmosphere and environment, while some deal with data and a complex set of information.

A diagram, a plan or a map are some of the visual vocabulary tools that architects use in a design/research process. The plan is a representation of a design or a proposal, it is a projection of a three-dimensional space, drawn in different scales, showing precise, detailed information. The plan, like the map, requires (technical) skills in drawing and reading. Another type of drawing is the "diagram", which exists across disciplines to compress and reduce information into a comprehensible visual format. It is an abstract, illustrative figure used to describe a scheme, a statement, a definition, a process, or an action, free from representational and typological restrictions. It is a translation of data into visual communication, without the connection to its geographical surface.

And as for a definition of "maps", matters get complicated. Maps remind us of the complexity of representing the world and its surface. There are multiple representations, depicting various realities. Maps are often easily mistaken for objective descriptions of geographical conditions, they are taken to be "true" and objective, as a measurement of the world. But maps are highly artificial, abstract and never objective. There is always an author (architect, geographer, planner, ...) who has selected, isolated and codified the space for certain reasons.

When we talk about mapping as a research method, this is not about the "pure" topographical map – the process of mapping is much more than describing surface. James Corner, in his essay "The Agency of Mapping: Speculation, Critique and Invention", describes the purpose and potential of mapping as a creative tool for a better understanding of spaces, cultures, and societies. Its opposite would be the traditional function of "tracing" geographies, tracing simply reproduces what is already known. In A Thousand Plateaus, Deleuze states: "What distinguishes the map from the tracing is that it is entirely oriented toward an experimentation in contact with the real."[2] According to Corner, our concept of space is formed by our participation with our surroundings. In this sense, mapping creates complex relationships to be visualised not only as a territorial but also as a sociocultural representation. So, is mapping a cultural intervention?

Maps describe characteristics of a particular territory (routes, built structures, land classification, ...) but when we talk about mapping as a research method, the quality of the map should never lose its spatial qualities and human interactions. Furthermore, the map can also show a narrative or indicate change and transformation. Maps can show unseen and often immaterial areas. Corner describes these as various

[1]
Ray Lucas, Research Methods for Architecture (London: Laurence King Publishing, 2016), 183.

[2]
Gilles Deleuze and Félix Guattari, A Thousand Plateaus: Capitalism and Schizophrenia (Minneapolis: University of Minnesota Press, 1987), 12.

[3]
James Corner, "The Agency of Mapping: Speculation, Critique and Invention," in Mappings, ed. Denis Cosgrove (London: Reaction Books, 1999), 214.

hidden forces like "[...], wind and sun, historical events, local stories, economic and legislative conditions, even political interests, regulatory mechanisms and programmatic structures." [3], which cannot be seen physically but influence the quality of a site. The map describes these various conditions and is still connected to the ground itself, making the landscape present as it exists and as it could be.
So, the map shows us both: what is given (topography, surface) and what will come (design).

The map is capable of describing existing and "imagined grounds". Through this benefit, mapping has the capacity to help us imagine fragments of new landscapes, cities and buildings. We can understand mapping as an instrument to imagine new realities, to propose alternatives and produce ideas and actions, which – in the best case – allow us to democratise imagination, creativity and in the end knowledge. It is time to apply mapping as a productive and liberating instrument in an architecture and design discourse, to unfold potentials, rethink territory and break new ground to imagine alternative futures.

The publication "Mapping the Croatian Coast" provides 8 folding poster maps by architecture students at the Vienna University of Technology. The maps try to investigate different phenomena of the Croatian Coast: for example new strategies for small villages along the coast, changes in mobility and transportation, metamorphosis and decay of hotel ruins, temporary housing structures and alternative concepts for tourism.
All topics are deeply connected to the ground, its surface, and the landscape. Even various hidden forces, like politics, law and ownership are mapped.

In all 8 maps, you will find new worlds within the past and the present; they reformulate what already exists and imagine and create new realities. Mapping has the potential to be a collective, cultural operation.

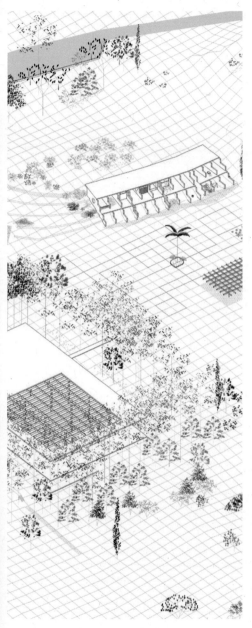

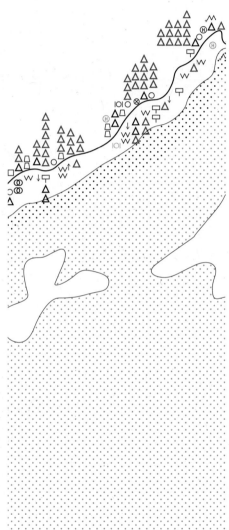

photo references historic photos

1 Archive photo
2 Historic postcard
3 Historic postcard
4 Haludovo original brochure, Brodokomerc Rijeka
5 CCN Images, Zagreb
6 Vitić Archive
7 Arhitektura, 196–199, Zagreb, 1986

8 Čovjek i prostor, 236, Zagreb, 1972
9 Original brochure of the Vitić design studio, 1967
10 Maria Groiss
11 Arhitektura, 196–199, 1986
12 Sušačka revija, 69, 2010, Rijeka
13 Historic postcard
14 Historic postcard

All illustrations ware made at the Research Unit of Housing and Design, if not labelled otherwise.

references travel guide

Ban, Saša, dir. Betonski spavači (eng. Slumbering Concrete). 2016. Zagreb: Hulahop for HRT, documentary series, 4 x 52 min.

Beyer, Elke, Anke Hagemann, and Michael Zinganel, eds. Holidays After The Fall. Seaside Architecture and Urbanism in Bulgaria and Croatia. Berlin: Jovis, 2013.

Bodrožić, Nataša, and Saša Šimpraga, eds. Motel Trogir: It Is Not Future that Always Comes After. Zagreb/ Eindhoven: Onomatopee, 2016.

Butković Mićin, Lidija. "Turistički biser Uvalu Scott treba zaštiti," pogledaj.to, October 22, 2014. http://pogledaj.to/arhitektura/turisticki-biser-uvalu-scott-treba-zastiti/.

Čavlović, Melita. "Constructing a Travel Landscape: A Case Study of the Sljeme Motels along the Adriatic Highway." Architectural Histories, no. 6 (2018): 1–14, https://doi.org/10.5334/ah.187.

Dika, Antonia. "Von Soldaten und Touristen. Verlassene Militäranlagen auf den adriatischen Inseln." Diploma thesis, Vienna University of Technology, 2008.

Dobrović, Ervin. "Dva nebodera – nacionalno i internacionalno u arhitekturi tridesetih godina u Rijeci i Sušaku viđeno u širem kontekstu." Peristil, no. 31-32 (1988/1989): 329–336.

Džeko, Nikolina: "Rikard Marasovićs Kindersanatorium in Krvavica. Bestandsaufnahme und Revitalisierung." Diploma thesis, Vienna University of Technology, 2014.

Gović, Vana. Andrija Čičin-Šain / Retrospektiva arhitektonskog opusa. Rijeka: Muzej grada Rijeke, 2009.

Grimmer, Vera. "Radikalnost dijaloga, Dom Armije Šibenik, 1960. / 1961." Arhitektura, no. 217 (2006): 79–93.

Ivanišin, Krunoslav, Wolfgang Thaler, and Ljiljana Blagojević. Dobrović in Dubrovnik. A Venture in Modern Architecture. Berlin: Jovis, 2015.

Kulić, Vladimir, Maroje Mrduljaš, and Wolfgang Thaler. Modernism In-Between. The Mediatory Architectures of Socialist Yugoslavia. Berlin: Jovis, 2012.

Lozzi Barković, Julija. "Hrvatski kulturni dom u Sušaku – prilog istraživanju i valorizaciji." Radovi Instituta za povijest umjetnosti, no. 29 (2005): 287–306.

Mrduljaš, Maroje. "Toward an Affordable Arcadia: The Evolution of Hotel Typologies in Yugoslavia 1960-1974." In Toward a Concrete Utopia: Architecture in Yugoslavia, 1948-1980, edited by Martino Stierli and Vladimir Kulić, 79–83. New York: MoMa, 2018.

Pasinović, Antoaneta. "Arhitektura hotela Solaris kraj Šibenika u svjetlu intenzivnije urbanizacije Jadrana." Čovjek i prostor, no. 189 (1968): 1–4.

Pavlović, Boro. "Turističko naselje u Uvali Scott kraj Kraljevice." Čovjek i prostor, no. 182, (1968): 1–3.

Rozić, Morana and Saša Šimpraga. "Umro je arhitekt Pelegrina," Vizkultura, September 11, 2018. https://vizkultura.hr/umro-je-arhitekt-pelegrina/.

Schwalba, Rastko. Igor Emili. Rijeka: Muzej grada Rijeke, 1999.

Venturini, Darko. "David Finci: Dva hotela u Kuparima." Arhitektura, no. 90 (1965): 45–48.

Further Reading

Hotel Recommendations

Nataša Bodrožić & Saša Šimpraga [eds]:
Motel Trogir: Nije uvijek budućnost ono što dolazi / It is not future that always comes after, Slobodne veze / Loose Associations, Onomatopee, Zagreb/Eindhoven, 2016

Brian Dillon [ed]:
Ruins, MIT Press/Whitechapel Gallery, Cambridge/London, 2011

Hannes Grandits, Karin Taylor [eds]:
Yugoslavia's Sunny Side: A History of Tourism in Socialism [1950s-1980s], Central European University Press, Budapest/New York, 2010

Christian Rapp, Nadia Rapp-Wimberger [eds]:
Österreichische Riviera. Wien entdeckt das Meer, Wien Museum, Czernin-Verlag, Vienna, 2013

Dylan Trigg: **The Aesthetics of Decay: Nothingness, Nostalgia and the Absence of Reason**, Peter Lang, New York, 2006

Elke Beyer, Anke Hagemann,
Michael Zinganel [eds]:
Holidays After The Fall. Seaside Architecture and Urbanism in Bulgaria and Croatia, Jovis, Berlin, 2013

Martino Stierli and Vladimir Kulić:
Toward a Concrete Utopia: Architecture in Yugoslavia, 1948-1980, MoMa, New York, 2018

Hotel Neboder
Ul. Strossmayerova 1, 51000, Rijeka, Croatia
t: +385 51 373 538
w: http://www.jadran-hoteli.hr/

Boutique Hostel Forum
Široka ulica 20, 23000, Zadar, Croatia
t: +385 23 253 031
w: http://en.hostelforumzadar.com

Hostel Goli&Bosi
Morpurgova poljana 2, 21000, Split, Croatia
t: +385 21 510 999
w: http://gollybossy.com/

Hotel Maestral
Filipinska bb, 21322 Brela, Croatia
t: +385 21 603 671
w: https://www.hotelmaestralbrela.com

–
European Emergency Number
112

field trip
along the croatian coast
October 2018

Irena Atanasova, Carina Bliem, Diana Contiu, Lucia de la Duena Sotelo,
Magdalena Drach, Aline Eriksson, Michaela Fodor, Sarah Gold, Raphael Gregorits,
Joana Gritsch, Maria Groiss, Nina Haider, Pia Knott, Cristina Krois, Philip Langer,
Michael Lindinger, Jakob Lugmayr, Manfred Wuits, Nina Zawosta, Marija Živanović
with **Antonia Dika, Bernadette Krejs** and our bus driver **Zoran Partalo**

Research Unit of Housing and Design
Institute of Architecture and Design, Vienna University of Technology

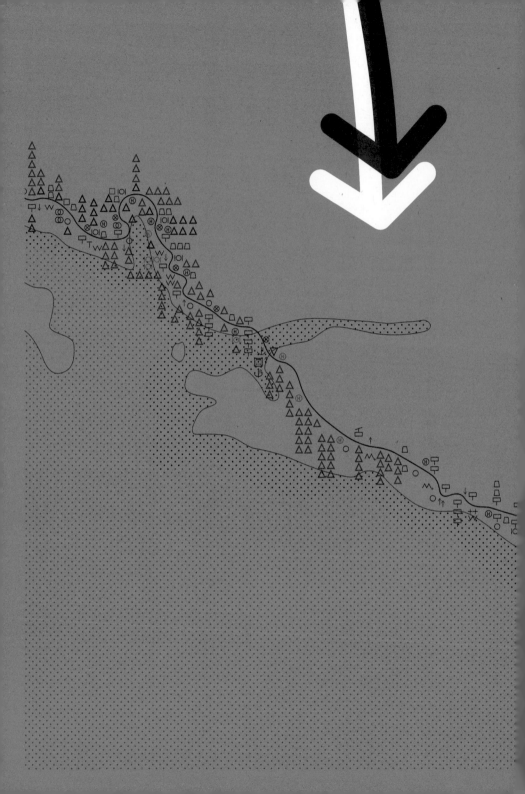

Mapping Jadranska Magistrala
Collective mapping, October 2018

⋀	Landscape
⋀₊	Beautiful landscape
⋀….	Beautiful coast
⋀	Landscape, Mountain
⋀	Landscape, Forest
⋀	Landscape, Forest, Mountain
✳	Landmark
+	Nice
++	Very nice
+++	Most beautiful
○	Town/Village/Settlement
∅	End of town
●	Buildings very dense
◕	Buildings dense
◑	Buildings quite dense
◔	Buildings sparse
⊓⊓	Isolated buildings
▽	Work
▽	Industry
⋁⋁	Agriculture, Plantations
⋁⋁….	Mussel bank, Fish farming
🐐	Goat farming
⊠	Public institutions [hospital, administrative buildings, …]
⊚	Community [public place, sports field, …]
☐	Shopping [mall, supermarket, …]
◧	Supermarket
▰	Mall
☐	Market
|O|	Restaurant, Coffee shop, Snack bar

P	Parking
P↙	Parking with a view
T	Filling station
Ⓗ	Bus stop
↓	Port
↓↓	Industrial port
↓P	Ferry port
✈	Airport
▣	Bus terminal
▤	Bus station
⊓	Cable car
↗	Military infrastructure
⊗	Street lighting
✗	Construction site
⊡	Ruin
?	Vacancy
†	Church
♱	Cemetery
▯	Streetart: Hajduk Split
⊓	Billboard
◿	Stone wall
↑	Road ascends
↓	Road descends
✗	Wind turbine

Dictionary
how to get in touch • fall in love • stay cool
en hr

Hello	Bok	**1**	jedan
How do you do	Dobar dan	**2**	dva
		3	tri
How are you?	Kako si?	**4**	četri
Thanks, fine.	Hvala, dobro.	**5**	pet
		6	šest
Goodbye	Doviđenja	**7**	sedam
Bye	Bok / Ćao	**8**	osam
		9	devet
Good evening	Dobro veče	**10**	deset
Good night	Laku noć	**100**	sto
Sleep well	Lijepo spavaj	**1000**	tisuću

Whats your name?	Kako se zoveš?	**black**	crna
My name is ...	Moje ime je ...	**white**	bijela
I am glad to ...	Drago mi je ...	**red**	crvena
		yellow	žuta
I love you	Volim te	**blue**	plava
When will we meet again?	Kada ćemo se opet vidjeti?	**green**	zelena

		right	desno
Please	Molim	**left**	lijevo
Thank you	Hvala	**straight**	ravno
Yes	Da	**behind**	iza
No	Ne	**here**	ovdje
Excuse me	Oprosti		

The bill please	Račun molim	**get in touch**	stupiti u kontakt
		fall in love	zaljubiti se
I do not speak Croatian	Ne govorim hrvatski	**stay cool**	ostati cool

I am an architecture student	Ja sam student arhitekture	**peace**	mir
		luck	sreća
		love	ljubav
I am vegetarian	Ja sam vegetarijanac	**life**	život

I am lactose intolerant	Ja ne podnosim laktozu
I am gluten intolerant	Ja ne podnosim gluten
I need a doctor...	Trebam liječnika

Imprint

This book was produced as a follow-up to the master design studio "Mapping the Croatian Coast", taught by Bernadette Krejs and Antonia Dika at the Research Unit of Housing and Design, Vienna University of Technology

253.2 Research Unit of Housing and Design [Prof. Michael Obrist, feld72]
Institute of Architecture and Design, Vienna University of Technology
A – 1040 Vienna, Karlsplatz 13 / 253.2 | www.wohnbau.tuwien.ac.at

Thanks to Anamarija Batista, Nataša Bodrožić, Jelena Barota,
[in alphabetical Matthias Brandstätter, Melita Čavlović, Diana Contiu, Milena Dika,
order] Aline Eriksson, Robert Antonio Graf, Joana Gritsch, Maria Groiss,
Nina Haider, Michael Klein, Antonia Kraus, Frida & Romi Krejs,
Igor Lebović, Inge Manka, Maroje Mrduljaš, Lidija Butković Mićin,
Michael Obrist, Franziska Orso, Vjeran Pavalković, Matthias Platzer,
Kristina Pliskovac, Brita Pohl, Sabine Pollak, Cäcilia Putschek,
Magdalena Reinberg, Helmut Schramm, Paul Sebesta,
Bruno & Raoul Steiner-Dika, Jakob Steiner, Manfred Wuits,
Lili Weissensteiner, Sylvia Winter, Michael Zinganel

Supported by Austrian Cultural Forum,
Faculty of Architecture and Planning, TU Wien
and Holzhausen, Gerin Druck GmbH

Editors Antonia Dika & Bernadette Krejs

Design and Setting Maria Groiss

Editorial Assistance Diana Contiu, Maria Groiss, Nina Haider

Collaboration Irena Atanasova, Carina Bliem, Diana Contiu, Magdalena Drach,
[design studio Lucia de la Duena Sotelo, Aline Eriksson, Michaela Fodor, Sarah Gold,
students] Raphael Gregorits, Joana Gritsch, Maria Groiss, Nina Haider, Pia Knott,
Cristina Krois, Philip Langer, Michael Lindinger, Jakob Lugmayr,
Nina Zawosta, Marija Živanović

Cover photo Maria Groiss

Proof-Reading Brita Pohl

Type Gravour Condensed

Printed in the European Union
Holzhausen, Gerin Druck GmbH, Wolkersdorf

Bibliographic information published by the Deutsche Nationalbibliothek
The Deutsche Nationalbibliothek lists this publication in the Deutsche
Nationalbibliografie; detailed bibliographic data are available on the
Internet at http://dnb.d-nb.de

jovis Verlag GmbH
Lützowstraße 33
10785 Berlin

www.jovis.de

jovis books are available worldwide in select bookstores. Please
contact your nearest bookseller or visit www.jovis.de for information
concerning your local distribution.

ISBN 978-3-86859-648-9